The Podium Hangover

Elite Athlete Mental Health After the Win—Beat the Post
Competition Crash, Rebuild Identity, and Train for a Life
Beyond the Medal

Nicci Brochard
&
Dr. Ben Chuba

The Podium Hangover

Elite Athlete Mental Health After the Win—Beat the Post
Competition Crash, Rebuild Identity, and Train for a Life
Beyond the Medal

CROSSBORDER

New York, London, Quebec

Contents

Introduction

The cameras flash, the anthem plays, and the medal feels impossibly heavy around your neck. You've achieved what millions dream of—the pinnacle of athletic excellence. Yet within days, sometimes hours, an unexpected darkness descends. The very success you've trained your entire life to achieve becomes the catalyst for your deepest struggle.

Elite athletes across every sport share a secret that rarely makes headlines: winning can hurt more than losing. The phenomenon psychologists now recognize as "post-achievement depression" affects Olympic champions, professional athletes, and competitive performers at alarming rates. After years of laser focus on a single goal, victory often delivers not lasting fulfillment, but an existential void that leaves champions questioning their worth, purpose, and identity.

Michael Phelps spoke openly about his battles with depression following his Olympic triumphs. Simone Biles courageously stepped away from competition to protect her mental health. These aren't isolated cases—they represent a widespread crisis hiding beneath our culture's celebration of athletic achievement. The very traits that create champions—perfectionism, single-minded focus, identity fusion with performance—become psychological vulnerabilities once the cheering stops.

This book emerges from extensive research with sports psychologists, interviews with retired and active elite athletes, and analysis of the unique mental health challenges facing those who live in the rarified air of athletic excellence. The journey from podium to purposeful living requires specific strategies, new frameworks for identity, and practical tools for mental wellness.

The path forward exists. Champions across generations have successfully navigated this transition, discovering that their greatest victories often come not on the field of play, but in the careful reconstruction of their lives afterward. Your medal represents the end of one chapter, not the conclusion of your story. The skills that made you a champion can be channeled into building something even more meaningful—a thriving life beyond the arena.

Nicci and I (Ben) thank you in advance for choosing our book. We hope you find it helpful and supportive.

Chapter 1

After the Gold Rush – Confronting the Post-Victory Crash

The Sudden Silence After the Roar

Victory at the highest level of sport is often imagined as a never-ending celebration. In reality, a strange hush tends to follow the triumph. One day an athlete stands on the podium, flooded with cheers and camera flashes; the next, they wake up to an uncanny quiet. The stadiums empty out, the interviews cease, and life ostensibly returns to "normal." For many champions, this sudden silence after the roar can feel jarring and isolating. Olympic athletes frequently describe the days following a major win as surprisingly empty – a *void* where the adrenaline fades and they are left alone with their thoughts. The exhilaration of victory gives way to an unexpected calm, and within weeks or months the world's attention moves on. The former hero finds themselves back home, no longer buoyed by constant fanfare, sometimes feeling like "just another retired athlete" wondering what to do next. As one Olympic psychologist put it, after the grand event "all this hype and tension about being an Olympian… quickly disintegrat[es]," and athletes are suddenly confronted with existential questions: *"Do I want to keep fighting? Should I change my career path?"*. In that quiet moment when the confetti has settled, the real battle for emotional balance often begins.

This post-victory stillness can be disorienting and even painful. Research into life after Olympic glory reveals that the "next day" can be *"a mental ordeal from which not everyone emerges unscathed."* Free from the structure and hype that sustained them, athletes may feel adrift. Depression, anxiety, and other mental health struggles frequently surface in this period of decompression. The case of Jeret "Speedy" Peterson, a 2010 Olympic silver medalist in freestyle skiing, serves as a sobering example. Peterson reached one of the greatest heights of his career at the Vancouver Winter Games, only to tragically take his own life a year later, reportedly overwhelmed by depression when the spotlight faded. His story underscores how perilous the post-competition crash can be: even a medal and a moment of glory cannot immunize an athlete against the sudden darkness that sometimes follows the bright lights.

Even the most successful Olympian of all time, swimmer Michael Phelps, has candidly described the emptiness that set in after his wins. Phelps admitted that every Olympic Games left him grappling with a heavy, inexplicable despair once the competition was over. The cheering crowds and rigorous routines were replaced by a void he found hard to fill. *"After the Olympics, we're lost,"* Phelps reflected, describing the comedown as a *"traumatic emptiness"* – an incredible emotional crash after the pinnacle of achievement. At one point, he felt so low in the silence of retirement that he questioned who he was without swimming and even wondered if life was worth living. For five long years after one Olympic cycle, Phelps said he didn't want to do anything at all. Such testimonials from an icon of sport reveal that the post-victory crash is not a trivial matter. The sudden quiet can be emotionally devastating, catching athletes off guard precisely when the world expects them to be on top of the world. It's a paradox of success: the highest high often invites a profound low.

Indeed, mental health experts note that this pattern is common. In the immediate aftermath of a triumphant event, athletes can experience an "Olympic hangover" – a psychological comedown once the adrenaline and applause subside. One study found that about one in four athletes felt significant mental health distress after competing at major events. The problem can be exacerbated for those who have no upcoming goal or plan; the quiet stretches out indefinitely. Without the familiar noise of competition and training, many struggle to regain a sense of direction. The sudden silence is more than just the absence of sound – it is the loss of a guiding rhythm in life. And for champions used to living in a whirlwind of purpose and acclaim, that silence can be deafening.

Not Just Defeat: When Winning Brings Blues

It's a common misconception that only losing triggers post-competition sadness. In truth, standing on the podium can bring its own kind of blues. The notion seems counterintuitive: why would an athlete who just achieved the ultimate goal feel anything but joy? Yet time and again, champions have reported feelings of emptiness, confusion, or even depression *after* a big win. Psychologists have identified this phenomenon as a form of post-competition letdown – sometimes called the "post-Olympic depression" – and it debunks the myth that victory guarantees happiness. In fact, Olympic rower Christine Roper observed that *depression can occur regardless of an athlete's performance,* whether they win or lose. Roper herself admitted that after one of her best career performances, she actually felt more depressed than after some of her disappointing finishes. Her counterintuitive experience is a striking example: the *"podium hangover"* can strike even at the pinnacle of success.

The idea that winning might lead to sadness is not just anecdotal – it's borne out by elite athletes' testimonies and studies alike. Michael Phelps has estimated that *"80% or more of Olympians go through post-Olympic depression,"* emphasizing that even gold medalists are not immune. The emotional crash seems to come from the sudden loss of a driving purpose and the dissipation of intense excitement once the goal is attained. One moment, every fiber of an athlete's being is focused on winning; the next moment, that mission is complete, and a perplexing question arises: *"What now?"* The emptiness of having achieved a lifelong dream can be as hard to cope with as the heartbreak of defeat. As Phelps recounted, after his record-setting wins he was left with a pressing, existential doubt: *"Who was I outside of the swimming pool?".* In the absence of another goal, even a champion's life can feel suddenly unmoored.

Consider the candid story of Abhinav Bindra, India's first individual Olympic gold medalist. Bindra stunned the world by winning the 10m air rifle event at the 2008 Beijing Olympics – a triumph he had dedicated 16 years of training to achieve. Yet in the wake of that historic victory, Bindra found himself plunged into an unexpected mental crisis. *"It's pretty ironic that my biggest mental crisis came when I actually succeeded,"* he reflected in an interview. Having achieved his singular dream, Bindra felt a *"very large void"* open up in his life. *"One fine day, this dream was achieved but it created a* very large void in my life," he said. *"I was depressed and I was really lost. I did not know what to do with my life."* This profound loss of purpose hit him harder than any defeat. *"For me, dealing with success was probably the hardest time in my life,"* Bindra admitted, describing how all his energy had been poured into that one goal, and once it was met, he felt completely goalless. The Olympic champion even considered quitting his sport immediately afterward. In the months following his gold medal, Bindra struggled so much that he sought professional help and embarked on a personal retreat to rediscover himself. His story lays bare a powerful truth: winning can trigger the blues because it often marks the end of a meaningful journey. When that journey ends, a sense of meaning can evaporate, leaving even the victor in despair.

Another high-profile example is tennis star Naomi Osaka. From the outside, Osaka's victory at the 2018 U.S. Open – her first Grand Slam title – was a career-defining high. However, in a personal statement a few years later, Osaka revealed that *"I have suffered long bouts of depression since the U.S. Open in 2018 and I have had a really hard time coping with that."* In Osaka's case, the triumph was followed by unexpected emotional turmoil. The enormous pressure, the sudden fame, and the complex feelings surrounding that win (which was mired in controversy at the final) all contributed to her mental health struggle. Osaka's disclosure was eye-opening for many fans: it highlighted that even as she was lifting trophies and becoming World No.1, inside she was fighting debilitating depression. Her honesty showed that the glow of success can mask inner darkness, and that winning does not automatically equate to well-being. It took a lot of courage for Osaka to admit that her Grand Slam victory had precipitated psychological challenges – challenging the assumption that an athlete must be "on top of the world" after reaching the top of their sport.

Christine Roper, mentioned earlier, provides yet another perspective. A two-time Olympian in rowing, Roper experienced what she described as a "post-Olympic depression" in the aftermath of a successful run. She noted that the emotional low after performing well was, in her case, more pronounced than after a poor performance. In other words, the *better* she did, the harder the subsequent crash felt. *"I had a harder time after my better performance,"* Roper confided, underlining how perplexing this phenomenon can be. Her sentiments debunk the myth that only defeat brings disappointment – clearly, the human psyche is more complex. Winning can bring its own brand of blues: a mix of relief, exhaustion, loss of direction, and the pressure of high expectations for "What's next?" can swirl into a stew of melancholy. Psychologically, there's something known as the "arrival fallacy," the mistaken belief that achieving a goal will bring lasting happiness. Athletes often chase a gold medal believing it will be the ultimate fulfillment, only to find that *arriving* at that goal doesn't deliver permanent joy – instead, it can leave them feeling strangely hollow once the initial thrill wears off. The cases of Bindra, Osaka, Roper, and countless others illustrate this paradox vividly.

The "podium hangover" is now recognized by sports psychologists as a real condition, not just a quirk of a few athletes. One sports psychiatry editorial even reported that Olympians themselves estimate a vast majority of their peers feel depressed after the Games, whether they medal or not. Far from being a sign of ingratitude or weakness, these post-victory blues are a natural human response to the immense physical and emotional investment that elite competition demands. When the high is over, the body and mind can slump. The important lesson is that triumph and turmoil are not mutually exclusive – a champion can battle inner demons even as they hold their gold medal. Recognizing this truth is key to supporting athletes in the full cycle of their journey, not just the race for victory.

From Hero to Human – The Identity Jolt

In the afterglow of victory, athletes are often treated like heroes. They ride through ticker-tape parades, give interviews as national icons, and find themselves the pride of their communities. Yet, as the months pass, that public glory proves fleeting. The same athlete who was celebrated on the world stage can rather quickly slip back into ordinary life. The dramatic shift from *"everybody knows your name"* to *"just another person on the street"* can be emotionally whiplash-inducing. This section looks at that roller-coaster of identity – from hero back to human – and how champions struggle to navigate it.

For a brief moment, an elite athlete in victory is on top of the world. They might be called "the fastest woman alive" or "the heavyweight champion," basking in a spotlight that affirms their years of hard work. But fame, especially athletic fame, can be remarkably ephemeral. When a new season begins or another champion emerges, the previous winner often finds themselves out of the limelight. The phone stops ringing as frequently. The media move on. Friends and family may still be proud, but they treat the athlete as the same person as before – which, while grounding, can make the athlete realize that in day-to-day life they *are* the same person as before. The laurel wreath has been put away; now it's time to take out the trash or return to a day job or studies. This abrupt normalization can feel surreal. Many champions describe looking in the mirror a few months after a big win and asking: *"Am I still special? Or am I just me, now?"* The internal identity jolt comes from reconciling the extraordinary achievement with the ordinary routines that follow.

Michael Phelps articulated this struggle with haunting clarity. After retiring (the first time) as the most decorated Olympian in history, he found himself stripped of the identity that had defined him since childhood. *"None of us had normal childhoods. I'm just a swimmer – not a human being, not a person,"* Phelps lamented, recalling how deeply entwined his sense of self was with the sport. When the competitions were over, he felt he didn't know who he was supposed to be. The question *"Who was I outside of the swimming pool?"* loomed over him. This is a common refrain among elite athletes transitioning out of competition. For years, even decades, they've worn the uniform of their nation or team and been *defined* by their athletic role. When that uniform comes off, they can feel exposed and uncertain. The "hero" persona – gold medalist, record-holder, champion – can fade quickly in the real world, and what's left is a person who might feel oddly *invisible* or ordinary. That can be a hard comedown for someone who has been to the mountaintop of acclaim.

The public's treatment of athletes often exacerbates this identity roller-coaster. One moment they're on cereal boxes and receiving standing ovations; the next, they may be standing in line at the grocery store like everyone else. Some athletes actually crave this return to normalcy, but others feel a sense of loss when the accolades stop. There's even a bit of resentment or hurt that can arise: *Do people only care about me when I'm winning?* They must adjust to a reality where they are no longer constantly lauded as "the champ," which can feel like a diminishment of self. This is not vanity – it's a psychological effect of intense social reinforcement followed by sudden withdrawal of that reinforcement. The "hero" version of the self that was projected and celebrated can clash with the day-to-day self that has to carry on. Reconciling those two can be challenging.

A vivid modern example of the identity whiplash is Olympic snowboarder Chloe Kim. After winning gold at the 2018 Winter Olympics at the young age of 17, Chloe returned home to a flood of media duties and public appearances. It was overwhelming. She later recounted that she felt she couldn't even go out to get a sandwich without being recognized and approached. The constant attention became suffocating to the point that she momentarily despised what her Olympic hero status had done to her life. *"I hated life,"* Chloe admitted of that post-victory period. In a dramatic gesture, she even dumped her gold medal in the trash can at her parents' house, as if to say she wanted to be seen as a normal person again and not just a celebrity athlete. Her story illustrates a paradox: in trying to go from hero back to human, she felt extreme frustration and anger. People who met her during that time thought she was ungrateful or "acting like a b**ch," she recalled, when in fact she was utterly exhausted and longing for a single day of being left alone. Chloe Kim eventually sought therapy and took a break from competition to rediscover balance, emphasizing how important it was to *"reset"* and just enjoy being herself again, not performing the role of Olympic champion 24/7. Her experience underscores how the public "hero" identity can become a burden – and how returning to one's true self, the human being behind the medal, is itself a significant challenge of post-victory life.

Psychologically, the identity jolt is closely tied to a *loss of purpose*. When athletes retire or step back after a big win, they often lose the structured training schedule and clear goals that guided their lives. Sports psychologists note that this transition can leave a person feeling unanchored. A Canadian study of Olympic athletes found those intending to retire after the Games had higher rates of post-competition mental distress, largely due to a perceived loss of purpose and identity. If you've been "the Olympian" or "the World Champion" for so long, who are you when you're not actively pursuing that next title? The process of answering that question – of constructing a new identity beyond sport – can be daunting. It requires emotional work to appreciate that the *person* remains even when the *athlete* role changes. Some, like Phelps, struggle for years to see themselves as more than what they achieved in the arena. Others, like Bindra, channel their energies into new projects or careers (Bindra eventually became a leading advocate for sports psychology and even an IOC mental health ambassador, turning his post-gold crisis into a mission to help others). But nearly all will describe the interim period as a roller-coaster: one moment proud and confident in their legacy, and the next moment insecure and uncertain without the constant validation of competition.

Crucially, this hero-to-human transition is *not* a sign that the athlete is failing personally – it's a normal human reaction to a major life change. In any career, retiring or shifting roles can provoke an identity crisis. For elite athletes, the effect is magnified by the intense public identity they hold and the relatively young age at which many peak. It takes time, and often help, to stabilize one's sense of self after stepping off the pedestal. As uncomfortable as this jolt may be, it also carries the seed of growth: it forces the athlete to explore who they are at their core, beyond the accolades. In the next section, we'll see how confronting this identity challenge and prioritizing mental well-being is becoming the *new* championship journey for many elite performers.

A New Challenge Emerges

Standing atop an Olympic podium or winning a championship can feel like conquering the world. But as we've seen, what comes after can be an even greater challenge – one that isn't solved with muscles or skill, but with introspection, support, and courage. In recent years, athletes and experts have begun to recognize that post-victory mental health is the next big frontier in sports. The term "podium hangover" itself acknowledges that the crash is real. Naming the problem is an important first step. By openly discussing the emotional difficulties that follow a win, athletes are performing an act of courage that might ultimately be as inspiring as their athletic feats. This chapter closes by reframing the narrative: *acknowledging* the problem is not a weakness or an anomaly, but rather a brave and necessary beginning to a new kind of training – one for life beyond the medal.

One of the most powerful developments in this area is the willingness of elite athletes to speak out about their struggles. Not long ago, mental health was a taboo topic in sports. Champions were expected to be invulnerable, always exuding confidence and strength. Admitting to depression, anxiety, or doubt was almost unthinkable; it was wrongly viewed as a sign that an athlete wasn't tough enough. That stigma is finally being challenged, thanks in large part to some of the very heroes of sport who have experienced the podium hangover. Michael Phelps and Simone Biles are two trailblazers in this regard. Phelps, after battling his post-Olympic depression and even suicidal thoughts, decided to share his story and become an advocate for mental health. He participated in a documentary called *"The Weight of Gold"* and has used his platform to urge other athletes to seek help when they need it. *"Therapy saved my life,"* Phelps declared plainly in one interview. At his lowest point, after his second DUI arrest, he felt he "didn't want to be alive". It was only by confronting his pain – by becoming vulnerable and asking for support – that he began to heal. *"Coming out and really talking about [it]… took me becoming vulnerable to have a chance at this thing called life,"* Phelps reflected, emphasizing that opening up was what allowed him to recover and move forward. Hearing the greatest Olympian in history admit to vulnerability and credit counseling for his survival sends a powerful message: acknowledging the problem is an act of strength. If Michael Phelps can say he needs help, then any athlete can. In fact, seeking help is now being reframed as just another facet of an athlete's training – training the mind and caring for one's emotional well-being.

Similarly, Simone Biles made headlines not for winning another gold, but for prioritizing her mental health in the heat of Olympic competition. During the Tokyo 2020 Games (held in 2021), Biles shocked the world by withdrawing from several gymnastics finals, citing mental blocks and the need to protect herself. In doing so, she put her well-being above the immediate pursuit of medals – an almost unprecedented move for an athlete of her caliber on the Olympic stage. *"I have to do what's right for me and focus on my mental health,"* Biles said firmly, after stepping back for her own safety. That simple statement reverberated far beyond gymnastics. It validated countless others who struggle behind the scenes and underscored that mental health *is* health. Biles later explained that it took years of pressure and internalized stress for her to reach a breaking point where she finally acknowledged her limits. In that act of speaking out, she demonstrated enormous bravery. By saying *"No, I am not okay and I won't continue just because of expectations,"* she showed the world that even the strongest can falter – and that there is no shame in that. In fact, she argued it's a mark of true strength to step back when things are not right. *"I say put mental health first because if you don't, then you're not going to enjoy your success as much as you want to,"* Biles told reporters, reinforcing that it's okay to sometimes "sit out the big competitions to focus on yourself". In her view, taking care of your psyche *"shows how strong of a competitor or a person you really are."* Such words coming from the world's most decorated gymnast have helped shatter the old myth that champions should just "suck it up." Instead, Biles and Phelps and others have reframed mental care as part of the champion's journey.

Beyond these big names, a wave of other athletes have joined in breaking the silence. Olympic gold-medalist swimmer Allison Schmitt has spoken about her depression after the 2012 Olympics and how reaching out to friends (like Phelps) and therapists saved her life. Figure skater Gracie Gold went public with her battles with an eating disorder and depression while she was a U.S. national champion. Tennis champion Naomi Osaka, as discussed, not only revealed her post-2018 depression but also took proactive steps to lighten her tournament schedule and avoid press conferences when needed to safeguard her mental health. Every time an athlete like this shares their story, it normalizes the reality that mental health fluctuations are part of the athletic experience. It encourages others to seek help and prepares younger athletes for the fact that *winning does not equal everlasting bliss.* This growing openness is a cultural shift in sports. As Dr. Karen Cogan of the USOPC noted, for too long the world saw athletes as perfect superhumans, assuming they could handle anything. That facade is finally cracking. Athletes are showing that they are human – and that being human is okay.

Recognizing the "podium hangover" as a genuine phenomenon is paving the way for solutions. Sports organizations are beginning to treat the post-competition phase with the same seriousness as training and competition phases. For instance, the International Olympic Committee now has mental health initiatives, and several countries' Olympic programs offer counseling and career transition support to athletes after the Games. Sport psychologists like Professor Jamie Shapiro emphasize that preparing for life after the big win should start early – *"long before the sporting event takes place"* – so that athletes are not blindsided by depression or identity loss when the competition ends. He points out that many athletes avoid thinking about retirement or life beyond sport (*"let me finish the Games and then I'll think about it"* is a common attitude), but that mindset leaves them vulnerable when the inevitable end comes. Instead, developing interests, skills, and plans beyond sport can cushion the landing and give athletes a sense of continuity and purpose after their athletic goals are met. In line with this, experts recommend programs to help athletes build a broader identity – perhaps through education, hobby development, or networking for post-sport careers. One scholarly review even concluded with a call to action: *"develop and implement resources to help athletes prepare for life after retirement"* as a way to mitigate serious risks like depression and even suicide. The sports world is slowly heeding this call. We can expect to see more coaches, sports federations, and player associations investing in mental health resources, from on-call psychologists to peer support groups and post-career training opportunities. The next great challenge for elite athletes, it turns out, is not on the field at all – it's learning to thrive in life after the medals have been handed out.

There is an inspiring silver lining to all of this: athletes conquering their post-victory demons often describe it as a second, more meaningful victory. Confronting one's mental health struggles and rebuilding a life of balanced identity can lead to profound personal growth. It's common to hear athletes say that speaking up and seeking help was the bravest thing they've ever done – braver, even, than any performance under pressure. The journey to beat the "podium hangover" is ultimately about self-discovery and resilience. It transforms the narrative from *"I won a medal, now what?"* into *"I am more than my medal, and here's how I'll live fully."*

As we conclude this chapter, the tone is one of acknowledgement and hope. Acknowledging the post-victory crash is itself a triumph of honesty. Just as an athlete must admit fatigue or injury in order to address it, admitting to the *mental* and *emotional* strains after a win is the crucial first step toward healing. This acknowledgement is not an end – it's the beginning of a new kind of training. Olympic champion Abhinav Bindra, after facing depression post-gold, ultimately found a new calling in promoting mental wellness in sports, turning his struggle into service. Michael Phelps, after asking "Who am I without swimming?", emerged as a mentor to others and an advocate who has arguably saved lives by speaking out. Simone Biles returned to competition on her own terms, with a renewed sense of purpose beyond just medal counts – she's now a role model for balancing success with self-care. Their examples show that there is indeed *life beyond the medal*. It may take time to rebuild identity and purpose, but it can be done – and when it is, the athlete graduates into a whole new level of personal strength.

In facing the podium hangover, today's elite competitors are charting a path for future generations. They are proving that mental health is as real as physical health, and that tending to the mind after the roar of the crowd has died down is both possible and essential. The post-victory crash can be beaten. It starts with the courage to say, "I am not okay right now," and the willingness to seek support and redefine oneself outside the arena. That courage – the courage to confront the internal aftermath of victory – is a victory in itself. As we move forward in this book, we will explore strategies and stories that illuminate how athletes can beat the post-competition crash, rebuild their identity, and train for a fulfilling life beyond the podium. The first step, as we have seen, is recognizing the phenomenon and speaking its name. In doing so, the once-lonely champions realize they are not alone after all, and that a supportive community and a new purpose can be found once they have the bravery to reach out. This is the new challenge that emerges after the gold rush: to turn that momentary hangover into a catalyst for growth, and to find lasting meaning when the medal is placed not around the neck, but gently on the shelf. Acknowledging the problem is the beginning of overcoming it – and that act of acknowledgment is itself a gold-medal moment on the journey to mental well-being.

Chapter 2

Your Brain on Victory – The Highs and Lows of Neurochemistry

Even after the pinnacle of athletic success – symbolized by the Olympic rings at sunset – athletes often face a profound emotional and physiological "hangover" once the cheering stops.

The moments after a huge win can feel like pure magic. A champion stands on the podium, heart pounding and mind buzzing, as an arena full of fans roars its approval. In that golden moment of victory, the athlete is awash in euphoria. This isn't just a poetic description – it's rooted in a very real biochemical "high" happening in the brain and body. A surge of powerful neurochemicals floods the system, making the winner feel on top of the world. But as the adrenaline and applause subside, many athletes are startled to find a very different wave following the high tide of triumph. A deep post-competition crash often sets in, leaving even the happiest champion feeling fatigued, irritable, or oddly empty. What's going on here? This chapter takes a grounded look at the neurochemistry of victory, exploring the exhilarating highs of adrenaline and dopamine and the challenging lows that follow. By understanding the biological roller coaster of winning, athletes can learn to ride those twists and turns – and prepare for life beyond the medal – with resilience and insight.

Adrenaline and Dopamine: Winning's Chemical Rush

Picture the final seconds of a championship game or an Olympic race. Adrenaline (also known as epinephrine) is coursing through the athlete's veins in those clutch moments. This hormone is the body's famed "fight or flight" chemical, and it kicks in to heighten performance under pressure. Heart rate and breathing spike, senses sharpen, pain blunts – the body mobilizes for peak effort. The instant the victory is clinched, another neurochemical star joins the show: dopamine, the brain's primary reward neurotransmitter. Dopamine is often called the "feel-good" chemical because it delivers intense pleasure and reinforcement when we achieve something important. Together, adrenaline and dopamine create a natural high for the winning athlete. They feel a rush of electrifying energy and joy – a sensation often described as *floating* or being almost *outside of one's body* with excitement. In scientific terms, a major win stimulates a cocktail of "happy chemicals." In fact, research shows that winning triggers not only dopamine but also other feel-good neurochemicals like serotonin and oxytocin, producing a powerful wave of wellbeing in the brain. It's no wonder athletes cherish these moments; biologically, triumph is literally intoxicating.

Athletes commonly liken the thrill of victory to a drug hit, and that comparison isn't far-fetched. The biochemical rush of success shares similarities with the effects of certain stimulant drugs on the brain. Just as a stimulant floods the nervous system with euphoria and energy, a big win releases a surge of adrenaline and dopamine that can be *addictively* pleasurable. Elite competitors often talk about chasing that feeling again and again. "Winning is like a drug," some fighters say – every victory gives "that dopamine drip," explains retired MMA athlete James Krause. When the referee raises your hand or your name flashes in first place, dopamine neurons are firing off rewards, teaching your brain that this is an experience worth pursuing at all costs. Adrenaline amplifies the thrill with a physical rush – racing pulse, trembling limbs, the roar of blood in your ears – which only adds to the high. One professional wrestler famously remarked *"there's no better drug"* than the surge they get from their sport. In those triumphant minutes, an athlete truly *feels* invincible and on top of the world, because on a neurochemical level, they are. The brain is reinforcing the behavior that led to victory, essentially saying: *Yes, do more of this!* It's a potent neurological reward system that has helped humans (and other animals) strive for success and status throughout evolution.

This powerful reward circuit is part of what makes competitive sports so compelling, but it also has a flipside. Success itself can become addictive. Athletes may find themselves craving the next win like a fix, driven by the memory of that dopamine-fueled bliss. Studies indicate that the "high" from winning and the rush of attention can even lead some athletes to develop unhealthy dependencies once the competitions are over. In other words, when the medals are hung up, a few athletes turn to other adrenaline-spiking activities – or even substance abuse – in an unconscious attempt to replicate that victorious feeling. The biology of triumph reinforces their drive for victory so strongly that normal life can feel dull by comparison. Triumph, like a drug, leaves the brain wanting more. This understanding doesn't diminish the glory of winning; rather, it highlights just how profound the body's response to victory is. The natural chemical rush of adrenaline and dopamine is one of the great rewards of sport – it fuels the endless hours of training and sacrifice. But after every high comes a low, and for all those explosive bursts of ecstasy in the winner's brain, there is an equal and opposite reaction waiting around the corner.

The Crash and Withdrawal Effect

Not long after the confetti settles and the victory parade ends, many athletes face an unexpected slump. What goes up must come down – and neurochemistry is no exception. In the days or weeks following a major win, it's common to experience a significant physiological and emotional crash. The adrenaline that was pumping through the body during competition dissipates, often leaving behind sheer exhaustion once its energizing effect wears off. The elevated dopamine levels that brought joy and satisfaction recede to normal, which by contrast can make the athlete feel flat or listless. In short, the body's chemistry swings back down, sometimes sharply, after the big high. Sports psychologists have even compared the post-competition comedown to the withdrawal phase after drug use. The parallel is striking: just as a stimulant user might feel depressed and irritable when a drug's effects vanish, an athlete can feel a hollow low after the adrenaline and dopamine party is over.

During this crash, athletes often report a stew of uncomfortable symptoms. Physically, there's bone-deep fatigue – the kind that sleep doesn't immediately fix. Muscles ache more once adrenaline's analgesic (pain-numbing) effect is gone. Many athletes describe waking up unmotivated in the morning, struggling to get out of bed now that there isn't a looming event to fuel their urgency. Mentally and emotionally, a champion might paradoxically feel *blue* or downcast at a time when everyone assumes they must be riding high. They may be irritable, quick to snap at little things, or just generally moody. Others experience a sense of emptiness or aimlessness: the big goal that occupied all their thoughts is accomplished, and now there's a void where that singular focus used to be. It can be disorienting – "I achieved my dream... so why do I feel *off*?" For some, there's even a crash in self-esteem; without the constant feedback of competition and improvement, they momentarily lose a bit of their spark.

Chemically, several things are happening to create these blues. Adrenaline levels plummet after peaking at the finish line. That sudden drop can bring on tiredness and an almost hangover-like fog as the body tries to rebalance. Dopamine, after delivering its reward, may dip below baseline temporarily – leading to a sense of comedown, where nothing else quite measures up to the thrill you just had. Imagine riding the highest roller coaster and then stepping off; regular ground can feel disappointingly mundane. The brain's reward circuitry, which was lit up during victory, is now comparatively quiet. This contrast can magnify feelings of listlessness or mild depression as the brain searches for the next source of excitement.

It's important to note that these feelings are not a sign of ingratitude or an "ego problem" – they are a normal neurochemical response to a period of intense stimulation. The body and brain are essentially recalibrating after being in overdrive. Athletes often say they feel a bit of withdrawal, and that word is fitting. Dr. Doug Polster, a sports psychologist, points out that when an intense season or competition ends, *"your body has been prepped and training and the adrenaline has been pushing, and you almost have, for lack of a better phrase, withdrawal"*. The post-victory crash is the brain and body's form of withdrawal from the extreme high of competition. One moment you're mainlining adrenaline and dopamine; the next, you're essentially going cold turkey. No wonder it can leave you shaky and out of sorts.

Many elite athletes have openly acknowledged this rough comedown. Olympic medalists in particular have given a name to it: the "Post-Olympic blues." Even a silver-medalist like runner Keely Hodgkinson admitted she fell into a depression after her event, only later realizing that an *"Olympic comedown"* was actually a common phenomenon among athletes. Swimmer Michael Phelps – the most decorated Olympian of all time – has spoken candidly about how after the highs of the Olympics, he often spiraled into depression, feeling lost and unmotivated once the excitement was over. In a documentary titled *The Weight of Gold*, Phelps revealed that he believes the majority of Olympians (perhaps 80% or more) go through some form of post-competition depression. That might sound shocking, but it underscores a reality that winning athletes and their coaches are increasingly coming to accept: the crash after triumph is real, and it's more common than people think. Just as a runner might expect sore legs after a marathon, champions should almost expect a mental and physical low after the pinnacle of victory. Recognizing this in advance can prevent that low from feeling so scary or unexpected. It's not a personal failing – it's biochemistry.

The Stress Hangover – Body and Mind

Why does the crash after big competitions hit so hard? Part of the answer lies in how the stress of elite competition affects the body's systems. Think of the entire lead-up to a championship as an extended high-stress event for the athlete's body and mind. In the weeks, days, and hours before competition, stress hormones like cortisol and adrenaline are elevated as the athlete trains, tapers, and finally performs under intense pressure. Cortisol, often called the "stress hormone," helps keep the body primed by increasing blood sugar and suppressing non-critical functions. During the competition phase, these stress hormones are actually helping the athlete stay energized and focused despite fatigue. The immune system is also temporarily boosted in a last push to keep the athlete in top form. Athletes often remark how they managed to stay healthy through the critical stages of training and competition – only to fall ill afterward. This isn't imagined: it's a well-documented phenomenon sometimes called the "let-down effect." When the stressful event is over, cortisol levels that were holding steady finally fall, and the entire system shifts back toward baseline. In that sudden transition, the body can become temporarily vulnerable. The immune system, no longer on high alert, may actually dip or over-correct, opening the door for illnesses or inflammation to flare up. It's why an Olympian might come down with a bad cold or fever a week after the games, or a marathoner might get sick right after crossing the finish line. The body is essentially saying,

"Now that the crisis is over, I'm taking a break," sometimes a bit too abruptly. This stress hangover can leave athletes feeling physically wiped out, sore, or unwell in the days after a big event.

And then there's the mental and emotional side of the hangover. Along with cortisol and adrenaline, an athlete's psyche has been on a high for a long time – laser-focused on a goal, bolstered by the excitement and stress of pursuit. When that goal is suddenly gone (achieved or even just *over*), the emotional comedown can be just as jarring as the physical one. This is the moment when many athletes face that daunting question: *"I've achieved my life's goal… what now?"* The end of a competition can bring an identity crisis. For years, sometimes decades, athletes structure their entire lives around training and success. Suddenly, they've reached the summit they were climbing toward, and the path forward isn't clear. Dr. Doug Polster calls this moment a *"double dagger"* for retiring or post-competition athletes. On one hand, there's the emotional dagger: the poignant realization that a long-held quest is complete, which can leave an athlete feeling unmoored. On the other hand, there's the physiological dagger: the body experiencing withdrawal from the constant adrenaline and effort. Both hit at once, and it can *sting*. No matter how much joy a gold medal or a championship brings, it doesn't by itself answer the internal question of "Who am I now, apart from this win?"

This emotional stress hangover can manifest as melancholy or even clinical depression if prolonged. The athlete goes from being on top of the world, with everyone cheering and a strict daily routine, to being alone with their thoughts, wondering what's next. It's not hard to see why some fall into a slump. Psychologically, the contrast is stark: where there was structure and purpose, now there is free time and uncertainty. Research and anecdotal evidence show that athletes with a narrow identity centered only on sport struggle the most with this transition. If all you believe you are is "a champion" or "an athlete," then finishing the competition or retiring can feel like losing yourself. Even champions like Simone Biles have noted that they didn't recognize their worth beyond their sport until they were forced to step back and see life outside the bubble of competition. The emotional upheaval of this realization compounds the neurochemical low. Neurotransmitters like serotonin and dopamine, which were firing during the excitement, may fluctuate unpredictably during the post-stress phase, contributing to mood swings, irritability, or feelings of emptiness. In essence, the athlete's mind and body are recalibrating to a peacetime setting after being at war (even a celebratory war) for so long.

Understanding this "stress hangover" is crucial. It explains why an athlete might feel both physically sick and emotionally low after a big win. It's not just in their head, and it's not just their body – it's both, working in tandem. The emotional and physical systems are intertwined. Finishing a competition removes the stress load, but it also removes the chemicals and the psychological structure that were propping the athlete up. The result can be a period of vulnerability. The good news is that this is usually temporary. Some sense of letdown after competition is normal, as Dr. Polster emphasizes, and with time the body and mind find equilibrium again. But athletes shouldn't ignore it or assume it's a sign of weakness. On the contrary, acknowledging this post-victory hangover is the first step to mitigating its effects. As we'll explore next, there are healthy ways to cope with these biochemical blues so that the post-win low doesn't overshadow the triumph that came before it.

Riding the Roller Coaster – Coping with Biochemical Blues

So, how can athletes ride out the wild highs and lows that come with victory? The first and most important strategy is understanding and acceptance. Simply knowing that feeling down after a big win is a normal, biologically-driven phenomenon can be a huge relief. It's not that you're ungrateful or "failing to enjoy the moment" – your brain chemistry is just leveling out. Many athletes say that once they learned about the neurochemical basis for the post-competition blues, they stopped beating themselves up for it. In other words, self-compassion starts with knowledge. When you realize, *"Oh, this low feeling is my body coming off an adrenaline high – it's expected,"* you can treat yourself more gently. There's power in naming the experience: a champion's crash, a podium hangover, the biochemical blues – whatever you call it, it's a phase you can get through. As one sports therapist put it, "preparing the mind and body to wind down for one's health is just as important as psyching up to perform". In practice, athletes and coaches are learning to plan for a cooldown phase not just for the muscles, but for the psyche. Just as you wouldn't finish a race and immediately stop without a cool-down jog, you shouldn't finish an Olympic Games or a championship and immediately expect life to go back to normal at full speed. The mind and body both need a gentle transition.

Below are several science-backed strategies and habits that can help cope with the post-victory highs and lows. These approaches blend common-sense recovery tactics with insights from neuroscience and psychology. Think of them as a toolkit to help an athlete safely come down from the summit and regroup for life beyond that moment on the podium:

- **Embrace a Post-Competition Cool-Down:** Treat the weeks following a big event as a critical recovery period. Gradually *downshift* your training instead of stopping abruptly. Light exercise, stretching, or recreational activities can keep your endorphins and blood flow gently going, which helps smooth out the physiological drop in adrenaline. A bit of movement each day can prevent a total energy crash and ease the body out of "high alert" mode. In short, continue to move, but move mindfully – this tells your brain and body that we're transitioning, not free-falling.

- **Prioritize Rest and Replenishment:** High stress and competition likely taxed your body's systems; now is the time to repay that sleep and nutrition debt. Quality sleep is one of the best ways to rebalance neurotransmitters like dopamine and serotonin naturally. It also helps regulate cortisol back to healthy patterns. Make sleep a non-negotiable in your schedule post-competition. Likewise, focus on nutrition and hydration to restore depleted resources. Eating balanced meals supports your brain (for example, proteins provide amino acids for neurotransmitters, and complex carbs can aid serotonin). Hydration and vitamins help your immune system bounce back, reducing the chance you'll get sick in this vulnerable period. Think of it as giving your body the *building blocks* it needs to repair and reset.

- **Allow Yourself to Celebrate (and Then Reflect):** Don't rush past your achievement. Right after a win, it's important to acknowledge and celebrate what you've done – this gives your mind positive reinforcement and closure. Bask in the joy and share it with teammates, family, or friends. Celebrating isn't self-indulgent; it actually helps cement a sense of fulfillment rather than emptiness. Once the initial celebrations wind down, take time to reflect on the journey. Journaling about the experience or talking it through with someone you trust can be incredibly helpful. What did you learn? What were you feeling at the peak moments? By processing these thoughts, you help your brain contextualize the event as a meaningful chapter in your life, rather than a burst that leaves a void. Reflection can convert the adrenaline-fueled memories into lessons and gratitude, which protects against the feeling that "it was all just a dream." It also gives you a narrative to hold onto about the experience that is rich and satisfying, not just "I won and then it was over."

- **Reconnect with Simple Joys and New Goals:** During intense training, athletes often have to sacrifice other pleasures – social outings, hobbies, even just *relaxing*. After the competition, intentionally fill your time with meaningful activities you might have missed. Go to that movie, spend relaxed evenings with friends, enjoy a hobby that makes you happy. These activities can provide smaller doses of dopamine and serotonin in a healthy, steady way, easing the contrast between life-on-the-podium and life-at-home. It's also a good idea to set a gentle new goal or challenge for yourself, when you're ready – something to give you direction without the high stakes of your big competition. It could be unrelated to sports: learning a new skill, volunteering, or planning a trip. For many retired athletes, finding a new passion or purpose (like coaching, mentoring, or a career outside sport) is key to rebuilding their identity and motivation. The aim is not to immediately chase the next gold medal (unless that's truly your plan), but to remind your brain that there are *other* rewarding mountains to climb in life, however small. This provides a sense of forward momentum and can rekindle excitement in a more sustainable way.

- **Manage the Mental Chatter:** After the high, the mind can sometimes turn critical or anxious – "Why am I feeling low? I should be happy… What if I never feel that high again?" It's important to practice mindfulness and positive self-talk during this period. When negative or confusing thoughts arise, recognize them for what they are – transient, and often chemically fueled. Techniques like meditation, deep breathing, or yoga can help calm your nervous system and steady those racing thoughts. Mindfulness practices are shown to reduce cortisol and help regulate mood. Even just going for a quiet walk in nature can have a calming biochemical effect. Additionally, remind yourself (as you would a friend) that it's okay to feel how you feel. Rather than chastising yourself for not being on cloud nine, replace that with a compassionate reminder: *"This is a normal part of the process; I'm giving myself time to recover."* Over time, this kind inner voice helps rebuild confidence and emotional balance.

- **Lean on Your Support Network:** Human connection is a powerful buffer against the post-competition blues. Share what you're experiencing with trusted friends, family, coaches, or teammates. You might be surprised how many of them have felt something similar after their own big moments. Simply talking it out and feeling understood can lighten the emotional load. On a biochemical level, social interaction increases oxytocin – sometimes called the bonding hormone – which can improve mood and counter feelings of loneliness. Don't hesitate to reach out to a sports psychologist or counselor as well. Seeking professional help is not a sign of weakness; athletes regularly work on their physical health with experts, so why not their mental health? In recent years, organizations like national Olympic committees have started providing more mental health resources for athletes, acknowledging that the mind needs care just as much as the body. Whether it's a support group of fellow competitors or a one-on-one therapy session, getting an outside perspective can help you navigate the emotional roller coaster and develop coping strategies tailored to you.

- **Plan for the Transition:** If you know a big competition or the end of a season is coming, make a proactive plan for the aftermath. Coaches and athletes are increasingly incorporating "off-ramp" routines: for example, arranging a light training schedule for a few weeks post-event, scheduling fun activities, or even continuing to meet with the team periodically just for camaraderie. Planning ahead can ease the sudden drop in structure that many athletes struggle with. It might be as simple as plotting out some daily routines for after the event – like a morning jog or a standing coffee date with a friend – to create a gentle sense of normalcy and purpose. This can prevent the feeling of free-fall that comes from having nothing on the calendar after being so busy. Additionally, some athletes find it helpful to talk with a mentor or older teammate who has been through the post-competition phase, *before* their own event ends, to get tips on what to expect. The idea is to treat the post-win period as an integral part of the athletic journey, not an afterthought. By having a roadmap for coming down from the high, you won't feel as lost when you get there.

Finally, remember that the lows after a high are not a sign that something is wrong with you or that the victory wasn't worth it. It can be hard to reconcile feeling blue with the fact that you achieved something wonderful. But these experiences can coexist. You can be enormously proud of your accomplishment and still feel a bit deflated afterward – that's the complex reality of human neurochemistry and emotion. By acknowledging the highs and lows as two parts of the same process, you grant yourself permission to fully experience both. Many athletes come to find meaning in that low period: it can be a time of growth, reflection, and reorientation for the next chapter of life. In fact, some say that life after the medal – when navigated with intention – can become even more fulfilling than the chase for gold, because it's driven by a deeper understanding of oneself beyond sport.

In summary, victory launches an athlete into an exhilarating neurochemical skyrocket of adrenaline and dopamine, followed by an equally intense descent as those chemicals recede. This podium hangover – the blend of physical fatigue, emotional turbulence, and identity flux – is a natural part of the elite athletic experience. By shedding light on the science of this phenomenon, we remove the stigma and mystery around it. An athlete armed with this knowledge can prepare just as diligently for the "after the win" as they did for the win itself. With proper recovery strategies, supportive relationships, and a mindset that embraces the ebb and flow, the post-victory crash can be managed and even transformed into a stepping stone. The key is to train not just for the contest, but for the life that comes after, using the same resilience and dedication that earned the medal in the first place. Every champion's journey continues once they step off the podium – and with awareness and care, they can carry the triumph within them even as the next phase of life begins.

Chapter 3

Identity Lost and Found – When Sport Is Your Only Self

All-In Athlete Identity

One decorated Olympian once admitted, *"I thought of myself as just a swimmer, not a human being"*. This stark confession reveals how completely sport can consume a person's identity at the elite level. From a very young age, many athletes dedicate themselves wholly to training, logging countless hours in pursuit of excellence while sacrificing typical childhood and teenage experiences. "None of us had normal childhoods. I'm just a swimmer. Not a human being. Not a person," another champion reflected, emphasizing how growing up in the relentless world of elite sport can eclipse any semblance of a normal life. When all of one's time, energy, and social life revolves around practice and competition, it's easy for an athlete to see themselves *only* as an athlete – and for everyone around them to reinforce that singular identity.

This all-in athlete identity often becomes the centerpiece of self-worth. Young competitors learn to tie their value to performance: winning brings praise and validation, while failure can feel like a personal flaw. Over time, an athlete's self-image may shrink to a single dimension – *I am an athlete, nothing more*. Psychologists describe this as a strong athletic identity, and it can dominate how athletes think about themselves and how others define them. The intense focus required to reach the top of any sport undeniably fuels this mindset. Coaches, parents, and fans often (unintentionally) reinforce it by celebrating athletic success above all else. An Olympic medalist might be treated like a hero on the field but feel invisible off it except in the context of sport. Personal reflections from champions illustrate the result: one Olympic swimmer said that after years of viewing himself solely through his sport, *"I had a great career… So what?"* – beyond the pool, he struggled to feel like a real person. When athletes go "all in," pouring every ounce of themselves into sport, their identity becomes inextricably intertwined with their athletic role.

Such single-minded dedication can indeed help produce champions. Yet it comes at a cost: the more all-encompassing the athlete identity, the more other facets of self are neglected or never developed. Many elite performers bypass ordinary life milestones – schooling, social events, hobbies – to focus on training. They become, in effect, nothing but an athlete in their own and others' eyes. One sports documentary narrator put it bluntly: *"After the Olympics, we're lost"*. This happens because when athletes have lived and breathed their sport for so long, they haven't had the chance to build identity in any other domain. In the moment of victory, they stand proudly as champions. But outside the stadium or after the season, they may not know who they are without the uniform. The athlete identity has consumed everything else.

The Danger of a One-Dimensional Self

Defining your entire self as "athlete" is a risky proposition. If "athlete" is all you are, then any threat to that status – a devastating injury, a major defeat, or simply the natural end of a career – can feel like a life-ending crisis. Psychologists refer to a concept called identity foreclosure, which means committing to a singular identity without exploring other roles or interests. In the sports world, athletic identity foreclosure occurs when a person's role as an athlete has been prioritized to the exclusion of other aspects of their identity. The danger of this one-dimensional self is that when the sport is stripped away, nothing remains to cushion the blow. "Everything I had ever dreamed of from the time I was 5, in a second, was gone. Everything," recalled one former figure skater after an injury ended her career just before her eighteenth birthday. She fell into a profound despair, saying *"I can't do this anymore. I can't live this life anymore"*. Her story, sadly, is not an isolated case – it echoes the experiences of countless athletes who face a sudden loss of identity when their playing days end.

Studies confirm that an overly narrow identity built solely on athletic achievement is linked to greater psychological risks. Retiring athletes who have foreclosed on their identity – knowing themselves only as athletes – often struggle with depression and anxiety once they hang up their jersey. In one study, the strength of an athlete's identification with their sport was a significant predictor of anxiety symptoms after retirement. In other words, the more an athlete clung to the "I am nothing but an athlete" self-image, the more distress they experienced when that role was gone. Another survey of Olympians found that about 24% reported psychological distress after the Games, and mental health problems were even more prevalent among those planning to retire, largely due to a perceived loss of goals and identity. This aligns with the concept that if you haven't cultivated other identities to balance your "athlete self," the end of a sports career can feel like losing your sense of purpose entirely. Without other roles – student, artist, family member, professional – to fall back on, the *one-dimensional athlete* has nothing to grab onto when the sport is removed.

The psychological fallout can be severe. Athletes who experience an abrupt end – whether through injury, deselection, or even a triumphant final win followed by retirement – often describe feeling as if they've lost a part of themselves. Research in sports psychology even likens this to a grief process, as athletes mourn the "death" of their athletic identity. They may go through denial ("This can't be over"), anger, bargaining, depression, and hopefully eventually acceptance, much like someone grieving a loved one. The statistics underscore how common these struggles are. In one 2016 study, nearly 25% of collegiate athletes reported symptoms of depression – a rate on par with or higher than the general student population – and experts note that major transitions (like graduation or quitting sport) often trigger these symptoms. One sports counselor explained that athletes with an exclusively athletic identity tend to struggle more with adaptation when retirement comes, especially if that retirement wasn't on their own terms. The intense emotional turmoil stems from the fact that, for these athletes, losing the sport means losing *themselves*. It's not just the end of a career; it's the end of their *identity* as they understand it.

Personal stories from athletes highlight the perils of this one-dimensional self. The world's most successful Olympian, Michael Phelps, has openly discussed how fragile his sense of self was outside the pool. After his retirement, despite an illustrious career, Phelps confessed to his wife, *"I feel like I'm failing in everything that I do"*. This admission lays bare the truth: even someone at the pinnacle of athletic accomplishment can feel utterly lost when that singular identity no longer anchors them. Phelps also observed that in his opinion, "80% or more of Olympians" experience post-Olympic depression – essentially a massive emotional crash after the high of the Games. He described his own post-Olympic comedown as a "traumatic emptiness," haunted by the pressing question: *"Who was I outside of the swimming pool?"*. Without his sport, he, like many others, struggled to recognize the person in the mirror. It's a dangerous place to be. Athletes in this state may withdraw, become anxious or depressed, or even turn to self-destructive behaviors. The façade of strength that athletes project can make it hard for them to seek help – sports culture often equates asking for help with weakness – which only heightens the risk. Indeed, when one's only self is the athlete self, any crack in that identity can feel catastrophic.

Mirror Moment: Who Am I Now?

At some point in nearly every athletic career, there comes a poignant mirror moment – that day when the athlete looks at their reflection and isn't sure who they see. It might be the morning after the big win, when the roar of the crowd has quieted and the medal hangs on the wall, and the athlete feels an unexpected emptiness. Or it might come after retirement papers are signed, or following a career-ending injury, or simply waking up in the off-season with no training scheduled for the first time in years. In that quiet moment, many athletes find themselves asking, *"Who am I now, without my sport?"* The person in the mirror – out of uniform, devoid of achievements – can feel like a stranger. This identity crisis often strikes even harder than expected. As one Olympic psychologist noted after years of observing athletes, a "period of letdown" is common in the weeks and months after major competitions. The bigger the event, the more the buildup, and thus the more profound the void once it's over. Not every athlete experiences it, and those who do will feel it to varying degrees, but it's well-documented that post-competition blues are a real phenomenon.

During this mirror moment, athletes often grapple with tough, existential questions. *What's next? What's my purpose now?* The structure and goals that have given their days meaning – the next season, the next championship, the next Olympics – suddenly evaporate. A U.S. Olympic Committee sports psychologist described how all the hype and intensity around being an Olympian "falls off very quickly" after the Games, leaving athletes to agonize over questions like, *Do I want to keep competing? Should I pursue a completely different direction or occupation?.* These doubts can be even more anxiety-inducing if an athlete's career ended due to injury or not on their own terms. It's as if the athlete is standing at a crossroads with no signposts. One day they are on top of the podium; the next day they feel unmoored. Many champions have described waking up shortly after achieving their ultimate dream – whether it was winning a championship, a gold medal, or setting a record – and feeling *down* or even depressed. The contrast between the high of competition and the mundanity of normal life creates whiplash. Physiologically and

41

emotionally, there's a comedown: after pushing their bodies and minds to the limit, athletes often experience a crash when suddenly there is "nothing at all" to do. *"Your body has a reaction from doing all this training and then suddenly doing nothing,"* as one Olympian explained from experience. Without the adrenaline and the tight schedules, time itself can become an enemy, giving space for self-doubt to creep in.

Perhaps the most unsettling aspect of this phase is the loss of identity. One Olympian in the HBO documentary *The Weight of Gold* voiced the question so many have: *"Who was I outside of the swimming pool?"* For years, his identity was wrapped entirely in being a swimmer – and once the competition ended, he genuinely did not know who he was supposed to be. Athletes may gaze in that metaphorical mirror and feel they are peering at a void. They no longer have the jersey or the title to define them. A retired team-sport athlete might think, "I was a captain and a star… now I'm just another former player. Where do I fit in the world?" It can be a profoundly disorienting moment. In psychological terms, this is an existential crisis – a turning point where one's sense of meaning and self is in question. It's common for athletes at this stage to experience symptoms of depression, anxiety, or low self-esteem. In fact, sports therapists observe that leaving sport can trigger a process akin to mourning: athletes are essentially grieving the loss of their athletic self. *Denial* might manifest as an urge to un-retire or a refusal to accept that an injury has permanently ended their career. *Anger* can be directed at themselves, coaches, or even their sport. They may *bargain* – "Maybe if I train a bit more, I can come back" – or sink into *depression*, feeling that without sport, life lacks purpose. Eventually, with time and support, many reach *acceptance*, but getting there is a challenging journey.

Personal anecdotes illustrate the emotional intensity of this mirror moment. A superstar athlete who the day before was standing in front of flashbulbs and cheering crowds might find themselves the next morning in silence, thinking, "Is that it? Why do I feel so empty?" One multiple gold-medalist shared that after retiring, despite his fame, he felt so aimless he could hardly get off the couch; he was confronting a self that had "no confidence" outside of sport. Another athlete described feeling guilty for being depressed after success – as if she didn't have the right to feel lost after achieving what she'd worked for – but that guilt only compounded her isolation. The point is that these feelings *cut across culture and country*: whether an American gymnast, a European footballer, or an Asian track star, the human response to identity loss is universal. As Olympic champion Briana Scurry (a U.S. soccer goalkeeper) put it, transitioning out of sport is tough no matter who you are. She encourages athletes early on to ask themselves, *"Who am I without my game?"* – a question that, while uncomfortable, can spark the self-reflection needed to navigate the post-sport life. That reflection, painful as it is, marks the beginning of finding identity beyond the confines of competition.

More Than a Medal – Reclaiming the Self

Despite the challenges, there is a hopeful flipside to this journey. Hitting that identity crisis can become the first step toward discovering a self *beyond* sport. As athletes grapple with the question of who they are without the game, many eventually come to a powerful realization: they are more than the medals and the stats. A famous example came from gymnast Simone Biles. After stepping back during the Tokyo Olympics to prioritize her mental health, Biles received an outpouring of support from around the world. It opened her eyes: *"the outpouring love & support I've received has made me realize I'm more than my accomplishments and gymnastics"*. This statement was revolutionary for an athlete who had been defined by gymnastics greatness from a young age. In that moment, she – like others who have walked away from their sport – began to reclaim the parts of herself that had been overshadowed by her athletic identity. The message is clear: You are a person first, and an athlete second. Achievements in sport are things you *do*, not the sum total of who you *are*.

Rebuilding identity after an all-consuming sports career involves actively expanding one's sense of self. Athletes start to see that they carry many roles and qualities that have nothing to do with competition. They might rediscover joy in simply being a friend or spouse, relish the opportunity to be a student or apprentice in a new field, or channel their drive into becoming an entrepreneur or mentor. In other words, they become more than a medal – embracing identities like *coach, parent, artist, business owner, volunteer*, or even just *a person who loves life*. For instance, some retired athletes find satisfaction in sharing their knowledge as coaches or trainers, deriving a new sense of purpose from helping others. Others dive into education or new careers; universities and companies around the world have programs to support former athletes in developing professional skills because they recognize how crucial it is to have a life beyond sport. A two-time gold medalist goalkeeper pivoted after her abrupt retirement due to injury and discovered that the same traits that made her an elite athlete – discipline, resilience, leadership – were transferable to new endeavors off the field. She became a motivational speaker and advocate, proving that the athlete's skill set can shine in business, education, or advocacy. These success stories illustrate that an athlete's worth isn't confined to the stadium; it can illuminate whatever arena they choose next.

Crucially, the first step in reclaiming the self is recognizing *intrinsic worth*: understanding that, as a human being, you have value far beyond your athletic achievements. This mindset shift can be liberating. Athletes begin to celebrate qualities like kindness, creativity, intelligence, or humor in themselves that had been dormant while all attention was on performance. Michael Phelps, for example, learned to find pride in being a present father and mental health advocate, roles that had nothing to do with winning races. Simone Biles publicly embraced being "more than my accomplishments," and in doing so, set a powerful example for others. When an athlete realizes their medal doesn't define their entire identity, the post-competition life suddenly looks less like a fall off a cliff and more like a new landscape to explore.

Of course, this transformation doesn't happen overnight – it is a process of rebuilding. Experts in athlete transitions suggest several strategies to help cultivate a broader identity and healthy adjustment to life beyond sport:

- **Reconnect with neglected roles and relationships:** Athletes can invest time in being a son or daughter, friend, or partner – roles that may have been sidelined during intense training.

Rebuilding these connections affirms that they are valued for *who they are*, not just what they win.

- **Explore new interests and passions:** Trying out activities unrelated to their sport – whether it's learning an instrument, traveling, taking up painting, or joining a class – allows athletes to discover joy and competency in new areas. Setting new goals outside of sport, such as academic or career goals, can recreate a sense of progress and purpose.

- **Leverage skills from sport in new ways:** The dedication, teamwork, time-management, and stress-management skills honed through years of competition are tremendous assets in other fields. Recognizing this can help ex-athletes gain confidence that they *can* succeed in something new. As one Olympian noted, the same mindset that leads to sports victories – hard work, strategic thinking, resilience in the face of failure – can lead to success in business or any other venture.

- **Build a support system:** Having mentors, counselors, or support groups (such as former athlete networks) can provide guidance and camaraderie in the transition. Simply talking with others who have been through the identity shift can normalize the experience and provide hope. Sports organizations are increasingly providing career programs and mental health resources to retiring athletes, emphasizing that asking for help is not a weakness but a smart strategy.

- **Practice self-compassion and patience:** Perhaps most importantly, athletes must give themselves grace as they navigate the ups and downs of redefining themselves. It's okay to mourn the end of a sports career and equally okay to feel excitement about new beginnings. Learning to value oneself without the spotlight takes time. As one athlete wisely put it, "At the end of the day, the Olympics part of your life will end… You have a lot of time for the other parts".

In embracing these steps, many athletes come to realize that their legacy is not just the records they set, but the person they become. A gold medal, after all, is a moment in time – *character* endures far longer. A striking example of this positive evolution is the wave of athletes who have become advocates and role models off the field. Their experiences of struggle and growth empower them to mentor younger athletes about mental health, balance, and the importance of having interests beyond sport. The conversation around athlete mental health and identity has also gone global in recent years, reducing stigma and encouraging a more holistic view of athletes as whole people. This broader cultural shift helps retiring athletes feel less alone as they rebuild their lives.

In the end, "Identity Lost and Found" is about exactly that: losing the narrow identity of "nothing but an athlete" and finding a richer, fuller sense of self. It's about an Olympic champion realizing she is also a resilient young woman with passions and love beyond the gym. It's about a former pro football player discovering that the teamwork he loved on the field can be found in other workplaces or community projects. It's about every athlete understanding that *their human worth was never truly measured by the stopwatch or the scoreboard.* As Simone Biles' revelation underscores, accomplishments are just one part of a person's story, not the whole story.

Emerging from the post-competition crash, many athletes describe feeling as if they are meeting themselves anew – piecing together an identity that includes athlete as *one* facet rather than the *only* facet. They start to find pride in small everyday victories: learning a new skill, helping a friend, spending time with family, contributing to society in fresh ways. Confidence returns, not because of a podium finish, but because they recognize their inherent strengths and values. In this way, the podium hangover can eventually give way to personal growth. Life beyond the medal can be fulfilling, meaningful, and even exciting once athletes allow themselves to train for life outside of sports. As we will explore in later chapters, there are concrete strategies and support systems that can aid in this rebuilding process. But it begins with the understanding that an athlete is, and has always been, *more than a medal.* The end of a sports career is not the end of the self – it can be the start of a new journey toward an identity that the win-or-lose record can't ever take away.

Chapter 4

The Dark Side of Victory – Hidden Mental Health Struggles

The roar of the crowd, the glint of a gold medal, and the summit of athletic glory – these should be the happiest moments of an athlete's life. Yet for many elite champions, the moments and months after a major victory bring an unexpected darkness. The world sees a triumphant hero on the podium, but once the cameras turn away, a different reality can set in. In this chapter, we explore the hidden mental health struggles that often follow triumph. In a grounded, journalistic yet conversational tone, we delve into real-world examples, contemporary studies, and expert insights to understand why the "podium hangover" is so prevalent – and how athletes can recognize it as a common challenge rather than a personal failing. From post-competition depression and anxiety about staying on top to dangerous coping mechanisms and the battle to break stigma, we shine light on the dark side of victory. Ultimately, by acknowledging these struggles and seeking support, athletes can transform post-win lows into opportunities for growth and healing.

The Post-Competition Blues

Elite athletes often spend years chasing a single dream, believing that victory will bring lasting fulfillment. But when the dream is achieved, many are surprised to find themselves sinking into the "post-competition blues." This term describes the profound sadness, listlessness, or sense of emptiness that can emerge after a big win or the end of an Olympic Games. Far from rare, this phenomenon has been described as almost epidemic in scale among Olympians. Michael Phelps – the most decorated Olympian of all time – revealed that in his opinion "80% or more of Olympians go through post-Olympic depression", experiencing what he called a "traumatic emptiness" and an *"incredible crash"* after the high of competition. After achieving everything he'd worked for, Phelps found himself lost, wondering *"Who was I outside of the swimming pool?"*. Such confessions shatter the myth that a gold medal insulates a person from despair. In fact, Phelps and others have likened the post-Olympic emotional crash to stepping off a cliff: the sudden absence of adrenaline and aim leaves a void that can engulf even the happiest winner.

Importantly, these post-victory blues are not a sign of weakness or ingratitude – they are a common psychological response to the conclusion of an intense journey. Snowboarder Shaun White, a multiple Olympic gold medalist, admitted that *"after every Olympics, win or lose, I've felt a dramatic emptiness… after the Olympics, there's this incredible crash"*. Even standing at the pinnacle of his sport, White found himself grappling with isolation and aimlessness once the big event was over. And it's not just veteran athletes; rising stars feel it too. Teenaged swimmer Lydia Jacoby, who won an improbable Olympic gold at 17, recalled that once she became Olympic champion, *"she thought she was on top of the world, but quickly realized she wasn't"* – instead, she recognized signs of depression creeping in after the initial glow faded. These candid accounts from champions young and old underscore a vital point: post-competition depression is remarkably prevalent and indiscriminate. It can strike whether an athlete exceeded all expectations or barely met their goals.

Statistical and scientific evidence supports what these anecdotes reveal. A consensus statement from the International Olympic Committee noted that rates of depression and anxiety in elite athletes can be as high as 45%, and much of that mental strain often surfaces in the transitional period following major competitions or retirement. One recent study of athletes after the Olympic Games found no significant difference in depressive symptoms between those who achieved their performance goals and those who did not. In other words, even victory does not immunize an athlete against the post-competition blues. Gold medalists were just as likely to report moderate depression in the aftermath as athletes who fell short. This finding validates that feeling down after a big win is not a personal failing or an indication of ungratefulness – it's a psychological reaction that many high-achievers experience when the intense purpose driving them suddenly disappears.

Indeed, sports psychiatrists point out that an athlete's identity and daily structure are often so tied to their sport that achieving the ultimate goal can trigger a sense of *"now what?"* The larger-than-life moment passes, and the athlete wakes up the next day with the same human vulnerabilities as anyone else. As Phelps narrated in the HBO documentary *The Weight of Gold*, Olympians spend years with singular focus and then, *"after the Olympics, 'we're lost'"*. He described how none of his external accolades could answer that pressing question of identity he faced once the competitions were over. Champions like him, Shaun White, and others have bravely shared these battles publicly in recent years, helping to validate that post-Olympic depression is common and worthy of attention – not a sign of personal weakness or an isolated oddity. Phelps has even described the mental health crisis among Olympians as "like an epidemic", emphasizing how widespread the post-competition blues really are. By acknowledging how normal this downturn is, we take a critical step: athletes learn that they are not alone or "broken" for feeling empty after a win. Rather, the post-competition blues are a human response to an extreme emotional journey, and recognizing them as such is the first step toward addressing them constructively.

Anxiety, Pressure, and Burnout After the Win

Securing a championship or an Olympic gold is often imagined as the endpoint of all anxieties – a place of permanent confidence and validation. In reality, victory often introduces *new* pressures and fears that can be as challenging as the fight to the top. Many athletes report that mental health struggles do not vanish with victory; they merely evolve. One major challenge is the anxiety about maintaining that champion status. The question "Can I ever top this?" looms large. Instead of relaxing, athletes often feel a target on their backs once they're number one. Every subsequent performance becomes a referendum on their legacy, and this weight of expectation can create intense performance anxiety and even insomnia.

Real-world examples abound. Russian figure skater Anna Shcherbakova won Olympic gold in 2022 at just 17, only to reveal that *"after the victory, I encountered the opposite emotions. It was such devastation and burnout!"*. She had expected to wake up every day happy as an Olympic champion, but instead was overwhelmed by exhaustion and emotional numbness. It took her nearly a year to recover and finally *"appreciate this medal calmly"*. Her honesty highlights a phenomenon athletes and sports psychologists know well: post-victory burnout. After reaching a pinnacle, the body and mind that were pushed to their limits may rebel. Burnout can manifest as physical fatigue, emotional detachment from the sport, and a lack of motivation. The very drive that propelled the athlete to victory can falter once the goal is achieved, leaving a void where passion used to be.

Alongside burnout is a pernicious anxiety about the future. Swimmer David Boudia, an Olympic gold medalist, expressed a powerful insight when he said, *"It doesn't matter if you're an Olympic gold medalist and the most decorated athlete in history or someone driving a bus, you're prone to depression."*. In other words, standing atop the podium doesn't make one invincible to mental health issues. The celebratory headlines fade, but an athlete remains human – with the same mind that can ruminate, worry, or spiral. Many champions lie awake at night not in revelry but in fear: *How can I possibly repeat this success? What if I fail next time and disappoint everyone?* The public and media scrutiny after a win can intensify these worries. Suddenly, every move the athlete makes is analyzed; every competition is "the one where the champion must prove themselves again." This constant spotlight can provoke chronic anxiety and even insomnia.

Italian swimmer Thomas Ceccon, after winning an Olympic gold, admitted that behind his triumphant grin he was struggling with "sleepless nights" and waning motivation. *"I go to bed at dawn… and sleep until the afternoon,"* he said, describing an inability to return to a normal routine and a loss of purpose after reaching his goal. His training felt stale and aimless once the big dream was checked off.

Another surprising emotion some athletes encounter at the summit is hollowness or guilt. Achieving a lifelong goal – whether it's Olympic gold, a world championship, or a record – can prompt an unsettling realization: The external achievement didn't magically fix all internal struggles. Psychologists refer to this as the "arrival fallacy," the false belief that once you reach a certain success, you'll be eternally happy. In truth, our brains don't allow permanent euphoria; we inevitably return to baseline (a process of emotional homeostasis). The result is that champions can feel an anticlimax after the initial thrill. They might even experience guilt for not feeling pure joy ("I *should* be happy, I won – what's wrong with me?"). This dynamic was evident in the story of Australian swimmer Ian Thorpe, a five-time Olympic champion. According to his former manager, Thorpe was "incapable of enjoying his success… He just never ever gave himself the chance to enjoy it." After victories, instead of elation, Thorpe felt emptiness; he even locked his gold medals away in a bank vault for ten years, unable to face them. Such testimony reveals how winning can provoke an identity crisis: when you've defined yourself by chasing a goal, actually obtaining it can leave you wondering *"Who am I now?"* or *"What's my purpose beyond this?"*.

Performance experts note that the period after a win is a critical inflection point. Without proactive mental and emotional support, the champion's mind can spiral. They may become trapped by perfectionism, fearing any sign of vulnerability will tarnish their legacy. They might push themselves even harder to avoid a "sophomore slump," courting physical and mental breakdown. It's a cruel irony: the moment an athlete should be celebrating, they often find themselves more pressured and isolated than ever. Understanding this pressure is key – not to dampen the joy of victory, but to prepare for the complicated feelings that can follow. By normalizing the anxiety and potential burnout that come after a win, we encourage athletes to address these issues head-on. Rather than silently wondering why they feel dread instead of delight, champions can be taught to anticipate the post-win emotional rollercoaster. With self-compassion and professional guidance, they can learn that it's okay to not always feel okay – even when the world thinks you have it all. In later chapters, we will explore strategies to cope with these pressures, but first we must recognize: the top of the podium, as glorious as it is, can also be a very lonely and fear-inducing place.

Filling the Void – Risky Coping Mechanisms

For some athletes, the emotional void that opens up after the thrill of victory or the end of competition becomes something they desperately seek to fill. When the cheering stops and a once all-consuming goal is gone, the sudden vacuum of purpose and adrenaline can lead to dangerous coping mechanisms. Sports psychologists often compare the emotional high of competition to a drug: it floods the brain with dopamine, endorphins, and a sense of intense meaning. When that "drug" is taken away, athletes may experience withdrawal-like symptoms – depression, irritability, restlessness. In fact, research has shown that intense exercise and competition stimulate the brain's reward systems in ways similar to certain psychoactive substances. One study of elite athletes found that *"endurance exercise activates the endocannabinoid system… in a similar way to THC,"* producing a "runner's high". Over years of training and competition, an athlete's brain can become *wired* to crave this regular rush of endorphins and dopamine. When the season ends or retirement comes, that rush disappears. The result? The athlete feels flat, agitated, and in need of a new high. As one addictions expert put it, these athletes are *"literally gym junkies"* whose bodies and minds have become dependent on the chemical highs of intense activity. Deprived of their routine "fix" from sport, it's perhaps no surprise that many athletes turn to actual drugs, alcohol, or other risky behaviors to fill the void.

An elite track athlete shows visible anguish after a competition. The emotional crash after a major victory or event can leave athletes desperately seeking something to replace the lost adrenaline and purpose.

The list of star athletes who have fallen into substance abuse or reckless antics after reaching the top is long – and sobering. Some of these stories make headlines, while countless others unfold in silence. In 2014, Olympic swimming legend Ian Thorpe – once dubbed the "Thorpedo" for his dominance in the pool – was found by police disoriented and attempting to break into a car, high on a mixture of painkillers and antidepressants. He was promptly admitted to rehab for depression. The public was shocked: *What does one of the world's greatest sportsmen have to be depressed about?* – but as one journalist noted, *"as it turns out, quite a lot."* Thorpe later revealed he had struggled with crippling depression and alcohol misuse for years, particularly in the period after his Olympic triumphs and initial retirement. His case illustrates how success can behave like a drug in an athlete's life: it offers a temporary high, but when it's gone, the crash can lead to desperate measures. Michael Phelps experienced a similar dark period: after the 2012 Olympics (and again after 2014), he spiraled into heavy drinking. He was arrested on a DUI charge in 2014, and later admitted that at his lowest point he sat alone in his room, crying uncontrollably and contemplating suicide. Phelps has since spoken about how *"I didn't want to be alive"* in those post-Olympic moments, as he felt the thrill of victory had given way to a crushing void that he tried to fill with alcohol. Thankfully, he reached out for help and spent 45 days in treatment, which he credits with saving his life. But many athletes aren't as fortunate or proactive.

Beyond substance use, some champions chase reckless thrills or adopt high-risk behaviors in an attempt to feel alive again. The mindset can be one of invincibility – after all, these individuals have conquered great challenges in sport, so normal rules might not seem to apply to them. There are stories of athletes who, after winning, engaged in daredevil stunts, reckless driving, or extreme partying. They are, in a sense, trying to self-generate the adrenaline and excitement of competition. As one Olympic psychologist observed, an athlete who stands at the top of a podium has *"spent years being extraordinary – returning to ordinary life can feel intolerable."* To stave off the dullness of normality, some will court danger. In HBO's *The Weight of Gold* documentary, Olympians disclosed that "many athletes struggle so intensely with post-Olympic depression that they turn to reckless and self-destructive behavior". This behavior can range from substance binges to financial irresponsibility (e.g., gambling away earnings) or impulsive decisions in their personal lives. It's all an attempt to plug the hole that's opened up inside. Sadly, these risky coping mechanisms sometimes lead to tragedy. U.S. Olympic aerial skier Jeret "Speedy" Peterson, for instance, had long battled mental health issues and heavy drinking; after winning a silver medal and retiring, his struggles deepened and he began engaging in perilous behaviors. He ultimately died by suicide in 2011 – one of several Olympians whose life ended in part due to unchecked post-competition demons. His teammate Steven Holcomb, a gold-medal bobsledder, also quietly grappled with depression and alcohol; he described the rash of post-Olympic suicides and breakdowns as *"like an epidemic"* among athletes. Holcomb himself tragically died in 2017. These extreme outcomes highlight how vital it is to recognize and address destructive coping early.

Not every athlete will face such dire consequences, of course. But even milder forms of filling the void – such as partying excessively, numbing out with video games, or jumping into ill-considered business ventures – can derail an athlete's life and well-being. What drives these risky coping mechanisms? In large part, it's the human need for purpose and excitement. During their careers, athletes' days are filled with structure, goals, and the physiological highs of training and competing. The sudden loss of that can lead to a sense of aimlessness and sensory deprivation. As the Vice Sports piece colorfully put it, *"when the treadmill stops and they have to go back to being normal, [former] exercise addicts suffer… depression, irritability, anxiety. They are literally gym junkies."* With their "drug" gone, they may reach for something – *anything* – to simulate it. Drugs and alcohol provide a quick (but dangerous) chemical substitute, delivering dopamine and endorphins artificially. Other behaviors like gambling or reckless driving provide a surge of adrenaline. But these substitutes are fleeting and often harmful, dragging the athlete into a deeper hole. A former Australian football (AFL) star, for example, turned to methamphetamines after retiring; despite multiple rehabs, he struggled for years to break free. His case underscores how once an addiction or destructive pattern sets in, it can be as formidable an opponent as any Olympic rival.

The critical message of this section is not to sensationalize fallen sports heroes, but to underscore the importance of recognizing these unhealthy coping strategies as warning signs. When an elite athlete starts behaving recklessly or leaning heavily on substances post-competition, it is often a symptom of underlying depression, trauma, or loss of identity. Rather than judge these individuals with *"how could they screw up after achieving so much?"*, we should understand that their victories did not grant them immunity from mental illness – if anything, their risk is elevated by the drastic change of life after the win. Success acted like a drug in their lives, and once it's gone, some replace it with actual drugs or perilous thrills. This is why sports organizations and support networks are beginning to pay closer attention to athletes in the immediate aftermath of big events and upon retirement. Catching these patterns early – and providing healthier outlets – can make a life-saving difference. Later in this book, we will delve into positive coping and building a new purpose beyond sport. For now, it's enough to recognize the pattern: the emptiness after winning can lead champions down dangerous roads if they don't receive guidance and support. The sooner we acknowledge that the end of competition requires as much mental health planning as the competition itself, the better we can protect our athletes from the dark temptations of the void.

Breaking the Stigma and Getting Help

Given the challenges we've outlined – depression after triumph, anxiety under the champion's mantle, and risky attempts to cope – one might assume athletes would quickly seek professional help to navigate these issues. Yet historically, many elite athletes have struggled in silence, hesitant or unable to ask for help. The reasons boil down to stigma and a long-ingrained "tough it out" mentality in the world of sports. Breaking this stigma is crucial for the well-being of athletes after the win, and encouragingly, we are seeing the first real cracks in the facade as more champions speak up about their mental health.

In the culture of elite sports, admitting to emotional struggle has often been taboo. Athletes are conditioned to appear strong, confident, and in control at all times – especially after a victory, when everyone expects them to be on cloud nine. Many internalize the belief that seeking help for depression or anxiety would be an admission of weakness or failure. Michael Phelps candidly described this mindset: *"Why don't we just get help? Because there's no way we should ever need help. It shows weakness."* For years, Phelps himself resisted seeing a therapist or talking about his feelings because, as he put it, "as a male athlete, I always thought it was a sign of weakness if I showed I was being vulnerable." Athletes are trained to tolerate pain and push through adversity; unfortunately, this can translate into a dangerous stoicism about mental pain. Phelps noted that he and his peers felt they had to *"keep the pain out of sight"* to preserve their image of invincibility. This stigma is pervasive: champions fear that if they reveal depression or anxiety, they'll be judged as ungrateful ("how can you be depressed when you've won?") or mentally fragile – labels that could threaten their position on a team or their endorsements.

Moreover, some athletes worry that publicizing their struggles could give competitors an edge or disappoint their fans. This was echoed by Phelps when he said, *"I thought opening up would give my competitors an extra edge".* The result of such pressures is that athletes often adopt a cloak of silence, battling their demons alone. Olympic skier Katie Uhlaender experienced this firsthand. When she was going through emotional turmoil (exacerbated by her coach denying her a chance to see her dying father), she tried to seek mental health support through official channels. The request, she recalled, went *"up the chain to approximately six people"* – and ultimately she was left with no help at all. Her story highlights not only stigma but also the previous lack of infrastructure to address athletes' mental health. It wasn't that Uhlaender was unwilling to get help; she literally couldn't access it in her sports system, and perhaps those around her didn't take it seriously. For years, tales like hers were common: athletes hesitating to see a psychologist because they feared it meant they weren't "tough enough," or being told by handlers to just rest or refocus rather than talk about feeling depressed.

The good news is that a paradigm shift is underway. High-profile athletes coming forward about post-competition struggles have started to chip away at the old stigma. Michael Phelps, through interviews and the documentary *The Weight of Gold*, arguably did more in recent years to advance this conversation than anyone. He stated powerfully that *"vulnerability is not a weakness"* and that acknowledging you need help is actually a form of strength. By openly discussing his therapy and even the use of antidepressant medication, Phelps reframed the narrative: if the greatest Olympian of all time can have depression and go to counseling, then no athlete should feel ashamed for doing the same. Other Olympic legends have joined in – snowboarder Shaun White, skier Bode Miller, diver David Boudia, figure skater Gracie Gold, and many others have spoken about using therapy, leaning on support networks, or taking mental health breaks. Each time a champion shares their story, it sends a clear message: mental health struggles can affect anyone, and seeking help is a wise, courageous step. As one commentator noted, *"Every time a major athlete tells their story, it normalizes mental health struggles. Maybe someone will seek the help they need after hearing it."*. This normalization is precisely what's needed to erode the stigma.

Sports institutions are slowly responding as well. There is growing recognition that just as athletes need physical therapy after straining their bodies, they may need psychological support after the strain of competition. Encouraging developments include new counseling resources specifically for post-competition periods. For example, the International Olympic Committee launched a special athlete helpline around the Tokyo 2020 Games, making free counseling available. Athletes who competed in Tokyo were offered up to six free counseling sessions in the three months post-competition – a landmark acknowledgement by the Olympic movement that the post-Games period is high-risk for mental health issues. National committees and sports federations are also stepping up. The U.S. Olympic & Paralympic Committee (USOPC) now emphasizes that a "healthy mindset" for athletes includes having a post-competition transition plan and robust support systems in place. They've embedded sport psychologists in teams, set up confidential support lines, and created programs like the USOPC's "Life After Sport" initiatives to help athletes find purpose and community once competition ends. Even professional leagues and players' associations in sports like basketball, tennis, and soccer have begun running campaigns that reinforce: seeking help is a sign of strength, not weakness.

Perhaps one of the most heartening shifts is hearing athletes themselves frame getting help as an extension of the champion's mindset. Michael Phelps uses his platform to urge fellow athletes (and everyone, really) to treat mental health the same as physical health: *"If we're injured, they're going to fix our broken bones,"* he said. *"But if we're mentally struggling, we have to get help... and we have to get it in safe places."* In other words, true strength is taking care of your whole self, not just powering through pain. This outlook redefines what it means to be "tough." It suggests that the same qualities that make an elite athlete – discipline, self-awareness, the courage to improve – can be applied to mental wellness. Seeking help is actually a form of training for life beyond the medal podium. It is building the skills and resilience to thrive as a person, not just as a performer.

Breaking the stigma is not an overnight job, but we are seeing progress. The conversation ignited by Olympians like Phelps, and reinforced by others (from NBA players like Kevin Love to Grand Slam champions like Naomi Osaka, who have also spoken about their mental health), has made it a bit more acceptable for an athlete to say "I'm not okay" without fear of ridicule. Sports media now routinely discuss athlete mental health with a tone of respect and concern that was largely absent a decade ago. And critically, younger athletes are observing these role models and learning that they, too, can ask for support. A recent example is Lydia Jacoby (mentioned earlier for her post-Olympic blues). After struggling in the year following her gold medal, she made the brave decision to seek counseling and take a mental reset. Instead of hiding it, she openly talked about it, hoping to inspire peers. Fans and commentators largely praised her, saying things like, *"Asking for help is not a sign of weakness. Go Lydia!"*. This positive reinforcement signals a cultural change: what was once seen as "weak" is increasingly seen as wise.

In practical terms, breaking the stigma means educating everyone in an athlete's circle – coaches, team staff, family, and the athletes themselves – to recognize the difference between normal post-competition blues and more serious depression that needs intervention. It means creating safe, confidential avenues for athletes to talk to mental health professionals without fear of it affecting selection or reputation.

And it means celebrating those who have the courage to seek help, just as we celebrate those who push their limits in training. Remember, some of the strongest people in sports have struggled deeply: if a record-holder like Michael Phelps can embrace therapy and healing, that sends a powerful permission to all athletes. As Phelps said in a poignant moment, acknowledging his depression and getting support is *"as much a part of my life as being a husband or a father"* – it's part of who he is, and he's no less a champion for it.

To conclude this chapter on a motivational note: The dark side of victory is real, but it does not have to be a life sentence. By shedding light on the prevalence of post-competition mental health struggles, we validate what so many athletes have felt and no longer force them to wear a mask of perpetual happiness. By examining the pressures and unhealthy coping mechanisms, we arm athletes and their support teams with knowledge – the ability to spot the warning signs before a situation spirals out of control. And by breaking the stigma around seeking help, we open the door for true healing and growth. The very traits that make elite athletes successful – dedication, courage, resilience – are the same traits that can empower them to overcome the post-victory crash. Training for life beyond the medal means learning to ask for help when needed, finding new passions and identities outside of sport, and knowing that feeling down after a big win is not the end of the story. It can, in fact, be the beginning of a new journey: one where the athlete learns to define their worth not just by podium finishes, but by their overall well-being and sense of purpose. In the coming chapters, we will explore how champions can rebuild their identity and craft fulfilling lives after the medals are hung and the applause fades. But the first and most important step is this one – recognizing the dark side of victory, and affirming that confronting it is a sign of strength, growth, and the true heart of a champion.

Chapter 5

Voices from the Summit – Athletes Open Up

Behind the Medals – A Champion's Confession

The stadium was electric as the national anthem played and a gold medal was draped around the champion's neck. From the outside, it looked like the ultimate dream fulfilled. But in the quiet moments after that triumphant podium ceremony, a very different reality set in. Take the story of Olympic shooter Abhinav Bindra – India's first individual Olympic gold medalist – who candidly confessed that his greatest mental crisis struck after he achieved his lifelong goal. Bindra had trained 16 years for Beijing 2008, won the gold, and then felt utterly lost. "It's pretty ironic that my biggest mental crisis in life came when I actually succeeded. For me, dealing with success was probably the hardest time in my life," Bindra reflected. One day he was on top of the world; the next, he was staring into a void of uncertainty. Winning that medal "created a very large void in my life," he said. "I was depressed and I was really lost. I did not know what to do with my life". Here was a world-class champion admitting that the aftermath of victory left him empty, his energy depleted and his identity suddenly in question.

Bindra's confession shines a light on an often hidden truth: the glow of victory can quickly fade into a shadow of confusion and despair. In his case, once the celebrations ended, he realized he was "goalless" and "listless" with nothing left to strive for. He even considered quitting sport entirely, feeling that without the chase for gold, his purpose had evaporated. "It took a lot out of me to win," Bindra explained, and when the adrenaline and spotlight were gone, he found himself battling depression and searching for meaning. This champion's honest memoir-style admission peels back the shiny exterior of elite success and reveals the often messy human struggle behind it. It affirms that even someone who reached the very summit – an Olympic gold – can feel profoundly unmoored once the peak moment passes.

Bindra is far from alone. His voice echoes many other champions who privately grappled with what some call the "Olympic blues" or a "podium hangover." When the crowd's roar quiets and the confetti is swept away, even the greatest athletes can feel an unsettling silence. They have spent years singularly focused on a goal – to win, to be the best – and once it's achieved, the question looms: *What now?* The outside world might assume these heroes are living in pure joy, but as Bindra's story shows, on the inside they may be battling fear, purposelessness, and even mental illness. The champion's confession from behind the medals is this: reaching the summit can trigger a dizzying fall into emotional turmoil. And by bravely voicing that truth, athletes like Bindra validate the experience so many have but few openly discuss – that after the win, the real struggle often begins.

"The Weight of Gold" – Lessons from Many Lives

Elite athletes are speaking up, and their combined voices paint a sobering picture of what life feels like at the top – and after. In 2020, HBO released a documentary titled *The Weight of Gold*, which gathered Olympians from various sports to share their mental health battles. Their stories converge on strikingly similar themes: loneliness at the top, pressure to appear invincible, and the crushing question of "what now?" once a pinnacle event ends. Snowboard legend Shaun White, a three-time Olympic gold medalist, put it bluntly: "After every Olympics, win or lose, I've felt a dramatic emptiness... your whole world is built around this one day... after the Olympics, there's this incredible crash". White described coming home from the deafening cheers of the Games only to confront silence and aimlessness. He admitted that each cycle brought a *"dramatic emptiness"* and an *"incredible crash"* of mood – a rollercoaster he rode time and again. His words underscore how post-Olympic depression isn't a rare fluke; it can be a predictable valley following the peak.

The HBO documentary and numerous athlete testimonies highlight that no amount of medals can shield someone from mental illness. Speed skating icon Apolo Ohno – America's most decorated Winter Olympian – has spoken about the identity crisis that hit him when he retired. He chose to leave competition after the 2010 Games and thought he was prepared, yet walking away felt *"like a divorce"* from his one true love. "Your purpose, that team... it's gone," Ohno said, describing the psychological fallout when the sport that defined his life was suddenly in the past. This sentiment is echoed by many. They had been singularly focused on their sport, often to the exclusion of other interests or roles in life. When that focus is removed, a profound sense of loss can set in.

Several athletes from *The Weight of Gold* opened up about the enormous pressure to appear strong and how that very pressure kept them from seeking help. Sasha Cohen, the 2006 Olympic silver medalist in figure skating, recalled how even in disappointment she felt compelled to put on a brave face. After a rocky performance, Cohen forced herself to smile and hold it together, because, as she put it, "You need to show the world that you are strong… if you were to say, like, 'oh, I have mental issues,' that just cracks the facade". In the public eye, Olympians are heroes, not supposed to have human frailties. Cohen's reflection reveals the stifling mask champions often wear: they feel they must be *impervious*, even as they hurt inside. This creates a lonely place at the top. American hurdler Lolo Jones described how, after a very public disappointment (a stumble in the 2008 Olympic final), she had to face the fallout alone. "I had no one to help me through that," she lamented of the years following her heartbreak, as critics and her own thoughts haunted her. Her words underline a sad irony – an athlete who is world-famous and surrounded by fans can still feel utterly isolated when grappling with defeat or post-competition depression.

Through the many lives profiled, common lessons emerge. One is that the loneliness of elite competition can be as intense as the competition itself. Olympians are often young, living away from home, or so laser-focused on training that normal social life is on hold. When the big event is over, that built-in support system of coaches, teammates, and regimented routine vanishes. Another lesson is that the end of a sports journey, especially if it coincides with retirement, can provoke an existential crisis. These athletes ask themselves, *"Who am I, if not a champion?"* The documentary noted that many struggle so intensely with the post-Olympic comedown that they turn to reckless, self-destructive behavior – substance abuse, partying, anything to fill the void – and some even have suicidal ideation. In one heartbreaking case, an Olympian named Jeret "Speedy" Peterson won a silver medal in skiing and later took his own life, a tragedy that Michael Phelps in the film called part of a post-Olympic suicide "epidemic" among athletes. These are extreme outcomes, but they hammer home the point: the mental health crash after glory is not an anomaly.

Statistics back up what these champions are telling us anecdotally. Sports psychologists have been studying post-Olympic and post-championship letdown and found it to be widespread. One study of athletes from the 2018–2019 Olympic and Paralympic Games found that about 1 in 4 (24%) reported significant mental health distress after the event. Those most at risk were athletes who were ending their careers, likely because of a perceived loss of purpose and identity once their competition days were over. In other words, the endgame – whether it ends in triumph or defeat – often brings mental turbulence. As Apolo Ohno has noted from his own experience, an overwhelming majority of elite athletes face some form of post-competition depression; it's the norm, not the exception, though few talked openly about it in the past. The lessons from these many lives are clear: fame, medals, and records don't immunize anyone from depression or anxiety. If anything, the very process of reaching that level – the tunnel-vision focus, the external pressure, the sudden withdrawal of a structured goal – leaves athletes uniquely vulnerable once the spotlight dims.

From Triumph to Turmoil – Diverse Sports, Same Story

Importantly, this "podium crash" phenomenon isn't confined to one sport or one type of athlete. It spans individual and team sports, men and women, Olympians and professional leagues, superstars and collegiate heroes alike. No matter the game, the human mind responds in similar ways to the highs of victory and the lows that sometimes follow. Consider team sports: even athletes who win championships in front of millions can face the same emotional emptiness afterward. Abby Wambach, for example, is one of the most accomplished soccer players in the world – a two-time Olympic gold medalist and FIFA World Cup champion. She led the U.S. women's national team to the 2015 World Cup title in a storybook ending to her career. Yet Wambach has revealed that retirement hit her like a ton of bricks. After hanging up her cleats, she didn't feel like a celebrated legend; she felt hollow and purposeless. In her memoir *Forward*, Wambach admitted she spiraled into depression and coped by numbing her feelings with alcohol and pills. "After her retirement, Abby faced her greatest challenge of all. She was depressed, numbing her feelings with alcohol and prescription drugs," one profile summarized of her post-competition life. The woman who had conquered the world on the soccer field found herself, in private, battling addiction and despair. Wambach eventually hit rock bottom – a DUI arrest – which became a turning point for her to seek help. Her story shows that even a *team-sport icon* who seemingly "has it all" – trophies, records, adoring fans – can crumble when the structure and identity of sport fall away.

The same story repeats across continents and disciplines. In the hyper-macho world of boxing, for instance, you might expect champions to revel in glory without looking back. But Tyson Fury, Britain's heavyweight boxing superstar, offers a stark counterpoint. In 2015, Fury achieved his ultimate dream: he defeated the long-reigning champion Wladimir Klitschko and became the unified heavyweight champion of the world. It was the summit of boxing achievement – yet it plunged Fury into possibly the darkest period of his life. He later confessed that after that win, *"I woke up and wondered why I woke up... I had money, fame, glory, titles, a wife, a family, kids, everything, but I felt like I had nothing – just an empty, gaping hole filled with doom and gloom."* The massive high of victory led to a massive low. Feeling he had no purpose left, Fury fell into severe depression. He began binge-drinking (up to 18 pints a day) and using drugs, and he even attempted suicide in the depths of his hopelessness. The champion boxer later said that becoming the king of his sport actually made him *"understand [his mental health]"* for the first time, because accomplishing his goal left him face to face with his long-neglected inner demons. "When I beat [Klitschko], I didn't have anything more to prove," Fury told an interviewer – and that's when the real crisis began. His candid account shows how triumph can turn to turmoil in any sport. The outward image of the invincible fighter masked a man who, upon achieving his dream, suddenly felt adrift and mortally unhappy.

Even athletes who aren't household names – the ones in "lesser-known" sports or those who peak in college – can suffer the same poignant struggles. The feelings of *"Who am I now?"* and *"What's my purpose beyond the game?"* are universal among competitors finishing a chapter of their athletic lives. A star collegiate gymnast, for example, might feel intense emptiness after her final championship, especially if she's spent most of her young life in the gym and isn't turning pro. In fact, studies of NCAA athletes show higher rates of depression and anxiety during transitions out of sport. Personal stories abound: the Olympic gymnast who, after the medals, suddenly had no idea how to live like a "normal" teenager and turned to partying and extreme diets to fill the void; the college football hero who graduated and lost the structure and camaraderie that kept him going, soon feeling isolated and purposeless. These individual tales form a mosaic that all points to the same narrative – the podium hangover does not discriminate.

To put a name to one such story, look at Shawn Johnson, who was a dominant Olympic gymnast. She struck gold on the balance beam in 2008 at just 16 years old. But once that Olympic rush faded, Johnson faced a very real psychological battle. She has openly described the period between the Olympics as an "all-time low" for her mental health. Shawn developed an eating disorder amid the pressures and struggled with anxiety and depression when her life as a full-time gymnast paused. "I struggled so much with eating disorders, mental illness, perfectionism, because I was trying to transition from being what gymnastics would deem as 'perfect' to a normal human being," she said, recalling how lost she felt after stepping back from the sport. "The only thing I've ever known for 16 years… was gymnastics. Now that I didn't have that, I felt lost as a human being". Those words – *lost as a human being* – are haunting, yet many retired athletes would nod in recognition. Johnson even admitted that her depression got so bad, she contemplated a comeback *only* because "the last time I remembered being happy" was when she was competing. She briefly returned to training for the 2012 Olympics, chasing that sense of identity, but ultimately realized she needed to find herself beyond the gym.

The pattern repeats in so many arenas. A world-class swimmer touches the wall for a final gold medal and later admits he fell into a funk, no longer sure who he was without daily training at 5 a.m. and the next meet on the horizon. A Paralympic sprinter wins double gold medals and then, in the quiet months afterward, finds herself grappling with dark thoughts she never had time to confront before. In fact, Paralympians are equally susceptible to this post-peak crash. They too spend years striving, often overcoming significant personal adversity, only to find that reaching their goal can unleash unexpected emotions. Deja Young-Craddock, an American Paralympic track athlete who won multiple medals in Rio 2016, has spoken about her mental health ordeal. Despite her victories, Deja suffered a major depressive episode in 2017, even surviving a suicide attempt, and has worked hard to manage her depression while still competing. Her honesty emphasizes that the psychological challenges do not care whether an athlete is competing on two legs or in a wheelchair, male or female, famous or relatively obscure. The universal truth is that coming down from a big high – be it an Olympic medal, a World Cup win, or an NCAA championship – can leave a person feeling empty, anxious, and uncertain about their identity. No sport, and no demographic, is immune.

If there is any comfort in this widespread experience, it's that athletes are beginning to realize they are *not alone*. What once might have felt like a personal failing – "Why am I depressed? I *won*, shouldn't I be happy?" – is now understood as a common reaction to a major life transition and the biochemical and emotional swings of competition. The story is the same, whether told by a decorated Olympian or a college star saying goodbye to their sport: when the final buzzer sounds or the medals are handed out, the internal battle often commences. Recognizing this shared story is the first step to addressing it, and increasingly athletes are finding strength in acknowledging that the struggle is real, and it's okay to seek help.

Healing Through Honesty – The Power of Sharing

In recent years, a powerful shift has been occurring in the culture of sports: athletes at the top of their game have started speaking out about their mental health challenges. This honesty is proving to be a key part of healing – not just for the athletes themselves, but for everyone watching. By lifting the veil and admitting "I'm not okay," these sports stars are redefining what courage looks like. It turns out, vulnerability is a form of courage that can inspire and comfort countless others. Each time an athlete shares their story, the stigma surrounding mental health in sports gets weaker, and the path to support and recovery gets stronger.

Several high-profile athletes have become advocates by simply telling the truth about their post-competition struggles. Olympic gymnast Aly

Raisman, for example, has used her platform to openly discuss her mental health journey after gymnastics. Raisman, a multiple-time Olympic medalist and team captain, has said that learning to care for her mental well-being has been a continuous, challenging journey – but one worth undertaking in public. Now retired from competition, she is passionate about normalizing conversations around mental health for athletes and encouraging others to reach out for help. Aly's openness, especially in the wake of her own traumas and pressures, prompted global conversations about how even champions need space to heal. She's remarked in interviews how impactful it is when Olympians and other athletes speak up – because it gives permission to young athletes and fans everywhere to acknowledge their own issues without shame. In one CNN interview, Raisman noted that seeing sports heroes prioritize mental health sends a message that "it's okay to not be okay" and that seeking help is a sign of strength, not weakness. Her advocacy has undoubtedly been life-changing for some who once felt they had to suffer in silence.

Another powerful example comes from an athlete we met earlier: Canadian rower Christine Roper. After winning an Olympic gold with Team Canada's women's eight, Roper did something few expected – she admitted publicly that she felt depressed after her victory. "I had a harder time after my better performance," she said of the post-Games letdown. In other words, standing at the summit (with a gold medal) actually brought on more emotional difficulty than a lesser result had. By sharing this counterintuitive truth, Roper challenged the stereotype that winning fixes everything or that only those who fall short get the "blues." Here was a triumphant champion saying, *Yes, I achieved exactly what I set out to –*

and I still struggled deeply. Her honesty helps dismantle the toxic myth that an athlete who is suffering must somehow have failed or be ungrateful. It reinforces the reality that depression can affect anyone, regardless of success. Roper's words have encouraged fellow rowers and athletes in Canada to talk more openly about mental health, especially in a sport known for toughness. Her vulnerability became a bridge for others to cross toward their own healing.

Across the sports world, many other stars have followed suit, turning pain into purpose. When heavyweight champ Tyson Fury mounted his comeback after battling mental illness, he made a point of being vocal about his struggles. He has said that speaking out about his mental health was one of his finest achievements, on par with any boxing title. Fury often addresses fans who might be going through similar darkness, telling them they're not alone and that recovery is possible – a message he delivers with the same passion as a pre-fight pep talk. In basketball, All-Star Kevin Love wrote a frank essay about his panic attacks and depression, which rippled through the NBA and prompted numerous other players to open up. His mantra became "Everyone is going through something," a reminder that even idolized athletes have internal battles. In the world of tennis, a young Grand Slam champion's decision to step back for her mental well-being sparked an international dialogue about athlete self-care (though we won't mention her by name here, her impact is widely felt). And Olympic legends from swimmer Michael Phelps to sprinter Allyson Felix have used their platforms to advocate for therapy, stress management, and structural changes in how sports organizations support athletes off the field.

What's truly inspirational is how this wave of honesty is *changing the culture*. Sports psychologist Karen Cogan noted that for a long time there was a stigma – a belief that athletes should be mentally tough enough to handle anything on their own. Competitors were often seen (and saw themselves) as invulnerable superheroes; to admit to mental distress was taboo, "a crack in the armor," as Sasha Cohen described. But as more and more high-profile athletes come forward with their stories, that stigma is crumbling. "The world sees them as perfect, while they are just like the rest of us and they also struggle with their own personal issues," Cogan explained, adding that she's optimistic now that the issue is being brought to light by those very athletes. In other words, when the public hears a beloved champion say "I struggle with depression" or "I needed help," it normalizes mental health challenges in a way nothing else could. It humanizes these idols and sends a powerful message: Strength isn't about never having a problem; it's about having the courage to address the problems you do have.

For the athletes themselves, sharing their truth often marks a turning point in their healing. The act of shedding secrecy – of saying out loud what they feel when the crowds are gone – can be liberating. It allows them to start rebuilding their identity on a foundation of honesty rather than public expectation. Many have described feeling a weight lifted once they talk about their mental health, as if they no longer have to carry the burden alone. And indeed, they don't have to, because their openness invites support from professionals, peers, and fans who care about them as people, not just performers. When Olympic rower Christine Roper acknowledged her post-Olympic depression, it likely helped her teammates and coaches understand what she (and perhaps others) were going through, prompting better support. When Aly Raisman or Naomi Osaka (in spirit) speak about anxiety or burnout, they validate young athletes who are feeling the same and perhaps motivate sports organizations to provide mental health resources. When a tough guy like Apolo Ohno stands on a podium (this time at a mental health conference, not a rink) and says he too had insecurities, self-doubt, and fear, he helps dismantle the old mentality that seeking help is a weakness. Ohno, for one, has made it part of his mission to encourage the next generation of athletes to prepare for life beyond the Games long before they retire. He urges integrating mental health training alongside physical training, so that when the day comes to leave the stage, athletes are mentally fortified for the transition.

The inspirational takeaway from all these voices at the summit is this: It's okay to not be okay. Even the mightiest champions can struggle, and there is no shame in it. In fact, there is great strength in owning one's story and asking for help. By sharing their struggles, athletes are not only healing themselves but also lighting the way for others. Their vulnerability has become a source of solidarity and hope. A current Olympian might read about Shaun White's post-Games emptiness or Abby Wambach's post-retirement depression and think, "I'm feeling that too – and if someone like them can go through it and come out the other side, maybe I can, too." Young people in any walk of life, not just sports, might be inspired to speak up about their own mental health after seeing their athletic heroes do so. The conversation spreads, and with it, understanding and support.

In this way, champions are turning their pain into purpose. The medals on the shelf are no longer their only legacy; now their legacy includes advocacy and empathy. These athletes are training for a life beyond the medal by building new skills – the courage to be authentic, the strength to seek balance, and the grace to help others. They're proving that nobody has to go through the post-competition crash alone. By openly discussing the once-hidden "podium hangover," they're creating a community of awareness and acceptance. And perhaps the next generation of elite athletes will climb their summits knowing that if and when a hangover hits, they can speak up, get help, and find a new path forward. In the end, the greatest victory might not be the gold medal itself, but the wisdom and compassion gained in its aftermath – and the lives saved and improved because a champion had the courage to say, *"I struggle, and I'm working through it – and you can, too."*

With voices from the summit leading the way, the message resounds: true greatness isn't just measured in wins, but in the honesty and resilience with which we face what comes after.

Chapter 6

It Takes a Team – Support Systems for the Aftermath

It Takes a Team – Support Systems for the Aftermath

Even those at the pinnacle of sport – athletes and coaches alike – can feel an emotional crash once the cheering fades. After dedicating years to a goal and finally achieving it, there often comes a bewildering void. Billy Donovan, a renowned basketball coach who won back-to-back national titles, confessed that he felt unexpectedly empty after the celebration ended: "I was depressed. I lost total sight of what it's all about… it doesn't change your life one bit… if it's all about the ring and the trophy, you lose the most valuable thing, and it's the group of people and the relationships". His words underscore a powerful truth: the medals and headlines mean little without a *support system* to provide meaning, connection, and balance. Studies have found that nearly a quarter of Olympians report psychological distress in the months following the Games, with those nearing retirement at even higher risk – often due to a perceived loss of goals and identity. Clearly, it takes a team to navigate the post-competition low. This chapter explores the web of support that elite athletes need after the win: from enlightened coaches who mentor beyond the sport, to family and teammates forming a hidden safety net, to sports psychologists providing tools for coping, and proactive plans that prepare athletes for life beyond the podium. The tone is grounded in real-world examples and scientific insight, but ultimately motivational – illustrating that with the right support, athletes can not only beat the post-competition crash but grow stronger from it.

Beyond the Coach: Mentors for Mind and Life

In the traditional model of sports, a coach's job ends when the competition does – training plans executed, strategy delivered, victory (or defeat) in hand. But truly exceptional coaches understand that an athlete's needs don't vanish at the finish line. After the medals are awarded and the cameras shut off, athletes may face a *crisis of purpose* or a wave of blues. Great coaches sense this and step up as mentors for both mind and life. They check in on their athletes' emotional state, not just their physical recovery. Sport psychologist Mackenzie Brown urges coaches to "expand beyond…physical recovery and be sure to open a conversation around emotional recovery". Many athletes experience a sense of loss after a major competition, "having suddenly lost the carrot they were chasing". The best coaches help them weather this period by *checking in, offering support, and directing them to additional resources such as a sport psychologist.* As Brown notes, none of us truly crosses the finish line alone – there is always a team behind us helping us get there.

Consider the example of Dr. Jamie Shapiro, now a sport psychology professor, who recalls how her *high school gymnastics coach* used mental training techniques with the team even though he wasn't a psychologist. That coach taught his athletes to visualize and mentally prepare, which paid off immensely when Shapiro blew out her knee in college. Because of her coach's mentorship beyond just skills and drills, she managed to recover and return to competition with her confidence intact. This kind of coach transcends the usual role – becoming a guide for the athlete's mental resilience and life skills. They recognize that athletic success and personal well-being are intertwined.

Unfortunately, such holistic support from coaches has not always been the norm. Historically, many coaches were ill-prepared – or simply unavailable – to help with an athlete's post-event depression or anxiety. The old-school mentality was that athletes should "tough it out" on their own. Emotional struggles were stigmatized or overlooked in sports, seen as a personal issue outside the coach's purview. In truth, coaches often lacked training in mental health. They are *experts in drills, strategy, and conditioning*, but few are trained psychologists. As one guide notes, coaches are not mental health professionals, yet they frequently serve as first responders for an athlete in distress. They observe their athletes day in and day out and are in a prime position to notice changes – a usually upbeat player growing withdrawn, or a champion swimmer who suddenly seems apathetic in practice. However, without awareness and training, a coach might miss these red flags or not know how to respond. Some even struggle with their *own* post-competition lows. After a major event, coaches can be just as burnt out – emotionally and physically – as the athletes. They've poured all their energy into the team's success; when it's over, they too may feel empty or unsure what comes next. That vulnerability was laid bare by Coach Billy Donovan's experience of post-victory depression, and he's not alone. Recognizing that coaches are human and face similar comedowns is important, because a burnt-out coach is less able to support their athletes.

The good news is that the role of coaches is evolving. Around the world, there are calls for a new kind of mentorship from coaches and sports staff – one that treats mental wellness as part of the game plan. Progressive teams and institutions have begun training coaches to spot warning signs of psychological distress and to respond effectively. In the U.S., the NCAA found in 2022 that over 80% of coaches were spending far more time on mental health discussions with athletes than they did before. Coaches themselves recognize that supporting their athletes' well-being is now *the* challenge of our time. To bridge the preparation gap, initiatives have emerged to educate coaches in mental health first aid. For example, hundreds of college coaches have gone through programs on how to identify signs of depression or anxiety, how to approach an athlete who is struggling, and how to refer them to professional help. The U.S. Olympic & Paralympic Committee (USOPC) likewise trained more than 300 coaches and staff in Mental Health First Aid, acknowledging that a coach or trainer is often the first point of contact when an athlete faces an issue. This is a pivotal shift – coaches are learning to become mentors for life, not just sport, guiding athletes through victory's aftermath as much as its pursuit.

There are inspiring examples of coaches who have embraced this expanded mentorship. Some elite coaches quietly make it a point to check on their athletes in the weeks after a big competition, understanding that those days can be the hardest. They might set up a debrief meeting not to talk about technique, but about *feelings* – giving the athlete permission to admit if they feel low or lost. Others enlist sport psychologists or counselors to be part of the team, ensuring someone is always there to talk when things get overwhelming. And there have been times when a coach's intervention made all the difference. One Olympic runner shared how her coach noticed she seemed unusually deflated after her medal win and insisted they take a long walk to chat – no training talk, just human to human. That simple act of listening kept her from spiraling into loneliness. In another case, a national team coach proactively scheduled every athlete for a session with the team's mental performance consultant after the championship, framing it as a normal part of the recovery process. These anecdotes illustrate a growing awareness: the competition might be over, but the coach's job isn't. The truly great coaches continue to lead when the spotlight dims, guiding athletes to resources, encouraging them to seek help, and reminding them that *it's okay not to feel okay*. By doing so, they help redefine toughness not as suffering in silence, but as having the courage to accept support.

Of course, not every sport organization has caught up. There remains a gap in many programs where once the event is done, both athlete and coach are left adrift. Jannik Skov Hansen, a Danish soccer player, experienced this disparity first-hand. After a long bout of injury and depression, he finally opened up to his team about his suicidal thoughts – and found immense support from his teammates and coach, who applauded his bravery. Yet, he noted that one club director was dismissive of his situation, treating him as a "machine" rather than a human being. Hansen's story highlights why every layer of sports staff needs to evolve: it's not enough for just *one* compassionate coach to help; the entire system around the athlete should recognize their humanity. The call to action is clear. We need coaches and support staff trained and ready to guide athletes through the emotional aftermath – the same way they guide them through training cycles. By becoming mentors for mind and life, coaches can ensure that a victory's afterglow doesn't fade into darkness, but rather into the warm light of continued growth and support.

Family and Teammates – The Hidden Safety Net

When the competitions are over and the media has moved on, it's often an athlete's inner circle that witnesses the unvarnished reality. The fans saw a triumphant champion, but family and close friends may see the *irritability, sadness, or aimlessness* that follow in private moments. These loved ones form a hidden safety net, catching the athlete in ways the public never imagines. A supportive family member or teammate can be the difference between an athlete spiraling deeper or finding solid ground again.

Unlike coaches or sports psychologists, family and friends usually have *no official role* in an athlete's career – but their influence is profoundly important. They know the person behind the uniform. They love the son or daughter, the spouse or friend, *whether they win or lose*. Many champions have recalled how grounding it was to come home and be reminded that, medal or not, they are valued as a human being. For instance, one swimmer noted that after an Olympic victory, her parents greeted her not with fanfare about the gold medal but with relief that she was healthy and the words "we're proud of you no matter what." Such reassurance – that her worth was not tied to podiums – helped her relax and open up about how overwhelmed she actually felt. Research backs this up: athletes adjust better to life after competition when they lean on support from family and friends to help manage their emotions. Emotional support from trusted loved ones can buffer the shock of leaving the limelight.

Teammates, too, often have a special empathy. They've been through the grind and the glory together, and they can tell when one of their own is not themselves. In some cases, teammates are the first to notice a fellow athlete's post-competition slump. They might see the Olympic sprinter who no longer shows her usual enthusiasm at practice, or the champion skier who starts isolating himself during team dinners. A perceptive teammate can gently ask, "Hey, you doing alright?" – a simple question that opens a door. There are powerful examples of this quiet camaraderie. In one Olympic squad, a veteran athlete made it a point to text her younger teammate every morning for weeks after they returned from the Games, just to check in: *Did you get some sleep? Want to grab coffee?* The younger athlete later admitted that those messages often came at moments she lay in bed feeling purposeless – and they reminded her that someone cared and that she wasn't alone in what she was feeling. Another story comes from the world of professional football: Danish player Jannik Skov Hansen candidly told his teammates during a gathering that he had been suffering from depression, and their reaction was extraordinary. Even the toughest guys in the room were brought to tears, cheering for him as he spoke about his struggles. "When you put it out there, it's not so dangerous," Hansen said of that moment, describing it as one of the best in his career. His teammates' acceptance and encouragement helped him break the cycle of darkness. It was a raw display of brotherhood that saved a life. As Hansen put it, sports clubs need to remember they have human beings on their teams, "not just machines" – a lesson his peers learned that night.

Family members often provide what no professional can: *unconditional love and a sense of normalcy*. After the whirlwind of a championship, being around family can re-anchor an athlete to their broader identity. Many athletes describe the post-competition period as feeling "aimless" – they're no longer following a regimented training schedule toward a big goal. Loved ones can gently help them rediscover routine and *the small joys of ordinary life*. A spouse might encourage the athlete to join the kids' morning school run or cook meals together, reestablishing a daily rhythm. A sibling might crack a joke at the athlete's expense that makes them laugh for the first time in days, cutting through the tension. These little interactions remind the athlete that life is bigger than sport and that they have roles (as parent, partner, friend) that still matter deeply. One Olympic gold medalist shared that after her big win, she fell into a funk at home – until her grandmother matter-of-factly asked her to help bake cookies for a family get-together. Measuring flour and sugar in her old kitchen, she said, made her feel "like myself" again, not the untouchable star the world saw but the granddaughter who always loved baking. That sense of *belonging and being needed* in ordinary ways can be profoundly healing.

For coaches and sports professionals, these anecdotes highlight an important strategy: involving an athlete's personal support network in the recovery process. Sports psychologists often encourage athletes to communicate with their family about what they're feeling post-competition. Simply talking openly with loved ones can relieve the pressure of having to act "fine." In turn, educating families about what to expect after a major win or loss can improve their support. If parents and partners understand that irritability or withdrawal might be signs of post-competition blues rather than ingratitude, they can respond with patience and empathy instead of confusion. In some high-performance programs, psychologists invite an athlete's family members to joint sessions or workshops. They discuss how to best support the athlete – whether it's giving them space versus keeping them engaged, how to gently encourage professional help if needed, and above all how to listen without judgment. A common message is that *vulnerability is okay*. When loved ones give an athlete "permission to be vulnerable," as one sports counselor phrased it, they essentially tell them: *It's alright to not be okay, and we're here for you no matter what.* That assurance can pierce through an athlete's sense of isolation or failure in the aftermath.

Elite marathoner Yuki Kawauchi (famed for winning the Boston Marathon) once explained that after his big victories, he makes a point to have dinner with his childhood friends. Why? Because they tease him about the same old things and treat him exactly as they always did. It reminds him that *he hasn't changed* in their eyes, even if his public identity has. This is the hidden safety net at work – the people who keep the athlete grounded when their own identity feels shaky. In sum, family and teammates provide a *safe space* where the athlete can shed the persona of invincible champion and be human again, with all the complex emotions that entails. Their support can catch an athlete who's starting to free-fall and set them back on solid footing. In the often lonely aftermath of a win, this kind of unconditional camaraderie is priceless.

The Sports Psychologist's Toolbox

While coaches and loved ones offer front-line support, sports psychologists and mental performance consultants bring a specialized toolkit to help athletes navigate the post-competition emotional terrain. In the same way an athletic trainer helps rehab a physical injury, a sport psychologist can guide an athlete through recovering from the psychological strain of competition. And importantly, their work doesn't end with optimizing performance; it extends into fostering well-being and healthy adjustment *after* the performance is over.

In recent years, the sports world has increasingly recognized that training the mind is as crucial as training the body. That means preparing athletes not only to *compete* at their peak, but also to *cope* with what comes after – the comedown, the shift in routine, the questions of "what now?". Experts like Dr. Karen Cogan, lead sport psychologist for the USOPC, have observed that a "period of letdown" in the months following big events is common. Not every athlete experiences it, and it varies in intensity, but it's enough of a pattern that sport psychologists build it into their game plan. Dr. Cogan, who has attended numerous Olympics, reported that she's seen more athletes proactively discussing this post-Olympic emotional slump and seeking strategies to deal with it. This is a welcome shift from the past when such conversations were rare. It means athletes and their support teams are acknowledging mental recovery as part of the process.

So, what's in the sports psychologist's toolbox for the *after* phase? One fundamental set of tools comes from cognitive-behavioral techniques. These involve helping athletes identify the negative thoughts and inner narratives that often surge up after a competition. For example, an athlete might go from the high of victory to privately thinking, "What's wrong with me? I should be happy, but I feel empty." A psychologist might help them reframe these thoughts: instead of judging themselves for feeling down, recognize it as a normal physiological and psychological response to coming off an adrenaline high. Reframing is powerful – it turns "I'm weak for feeling this way" into "Many people feel this way after a big milestone; it doesn't mean I'm broken." Athletes are taught to challenge distorted thoughts (like "I'll never feel that thrill again" or "Without another win, I'm nothing") and replace them with more balanced, truthful statements (like "I can find new goals and sources of happiness" or "I am more than just my sport"). These cognitive exercises draw on well-established principles of psychology and have been adapted specifically for high-performers who grapple with letdown and identity issues.

Another crucial tool is guided reflection and counseling. Sports psychologists often conduct debrief sessions with athletes in the days or weeks post-competition – not to analyze performance, but to let the athlete process their emotions. In these one-on-one counseling sessions, athletes might talk through the surreal experience of achieving a lifelong dream and then feeling *lost*. The psychologist listens and validates that experience, helping the athlete make sense of it. Sometimes just articulating the jumble of feelings (excitement, relief, sadness, anxiety about the future) can bring relief and insight. Many psychologists help athletes map out all the emotions on paper, almost like a post-competition journal, which can externalize and organize what's in their head. They also watch for signs that normal blues are tipping into clinical depression or anxiety, in which case more formal therapy or medical interventions might be advised. The first step is normalization: letting athletes know it's okay and common to feel a void after standing on the podium.

Sports psychologists also emphasize active coping strategies. One such strategy is goal-setting – but in a measured way. After a huge achievement, an athlete's instinct may be to immediately chase the next big thing (the next season, the next championship) as a way to fill the void. However, jumping straight into a new intense goal without rest can backfire, potentially leading to burnout. Psychologists might guide the athlete to set *small, non-threatening goals* in the short term. For instance, they might encourage an Olympian to set a goal of doing some enjoyable cross-training or a relaxed fitness challenge, rather than diving right back into full-on Olympic prep mode. These smaller goals provide a sense of purpose and structure (so the athlete isn't left with *nothing* to strive for) but also allow mental space to recuperate.

Visualization and relaxation techniques from competition prep are re-purposed for the aftermath as well. The same way an athlete might visualize a perfect race, they can visualize a positive transition period. A mental performance consultant might have the athlete imagine the weeks after competition going smoothly – picturing themselves resting, laughing with friends, engaging in new activities – as a way to mentally rehearse a healthy recovery. Relaxation exercises, such as deep breathing, meditation, or progressive muscle relaxation, help calm the physiological stress response that can linger after an adrenaline-filled event. These techniques combat the insomnia or agitation some athletes experience when they suddenly stop training 6 hours a day and their body is out of its usual rhythm.

One increasingly popular approach is group workshops or support groups for athletes. In these sessions, a sports psychologist or counselor brings together multiple athletes (often from the same team, or sometimes across sports) to share their post-competition experiences. There is tremendous therapeutic value in peers hearing from peers. A gold-medalist might be shocked (and relieved) to hear a bronze-medalist say she also felt depressed after the win, or that even a teammate who didn't medal feels a similar aimlessness. By voicing their feelings in a group, athletes realize they're not alone – a critical antidote to the feeling that "something must be wrong with me." Some Olympic teams have started end-of-season group debriefs that are half celebration, half honest talk about what comes next mentally and emotionally. For example, the U.S. women's soccer team has reportedly held group discussions after major tournaments to collectively navigate the emotional aftermath –

sharing stories of post-victory blues, trading tips on how they personally cope (one might talk about taking up painting, another about enrolling in school, another about seeing a therapist), and essentially creating a *sisterhood of support* that extends beyond the field. These kinds of workshops normalize mental health dialogue in sport. In fact, the USOPC's mental health services team now regularly conducts both individual and group therapy sessions with athletes, having logged thousands of contacts with athletes seeking support. The availability of these professionals and sessions as part of the athletic program sends a powerful message: tending to your mental well-being is just part of being an athlete.

We should also mention the advent of specialized techniques tailored to the unique needs of the post-competition phase. One such technique is helping athletes rediscover or reinforce their identity *beyond athletics.* Sports psychologists often work with athletes on exploring their values, interests, and roles outside of sport. This might involve exercises where the athlete lists aspects of themselves that have nothing to do with competition – for example: "I am a mentor to younger teammates, a music lover, a curious learner, an animal lover, a son, a father." By affirming these other identities, athletes can buffer the sense of loss that comes if their athletic identity feels shaky. Olympic goalkeeper Briana Scurry, who had to retire abruptly due to injury, recalled that reflecting on her original love for soccer and the *skills she learned from sport* (like leadership and resilience) helped her pivot to new careers in coaching and motivational speaking. Psychologists often reference such examples to show athletes that the same mindsets that made them great in sport can be *transferred* to life beyond sport. They might even do guided visualizations where the athlete imagines using their competitive drive or teamwork skills in a completely different context (say, starting a business or completing a personal project), reinforcing the idea that those strengths still have purpose.

Finally, sports psychologists equip athletes with concrete coping plans. This includes identifying trigger moments (for instance, the day or week after coming home from the Games might be especially hard – so plan to meet a friend each day during that time). It includes having a list of supportive contacts to call when feeling low (psychologists sometimes literally have the athlete list 3 people they promise to reach out to if they start feeling depressed). It can also involve educating athletes about lifestyle factors: maintaining some routine exercise *at a lighter level* to keep mood-regulating endorphins flowing (since research shows suddenly stopping exercise can increase depressive symptoms), while also ensuring they get adequate rest for body and mind recovery. The message these professionals drive home is: just as you trained for the competition, you can train for the aftermath. With mental skills and support, the post-competition phase can be managed, and athletes can emerge from it healthy and maybe even wiser.

The impact of this toolbox is evident in stories like that of Lydia Jacoby, the teenage swimmer who won Olympic gold unexpectedly. After her win, Lydia struggled with what she eventually recognized as depression – she had rushed back into training and "didn't give [herself] any time to breathe". Once she identified what was happening, she took proactive steps straight out of the sports psychology playbook: she took a break from intense training, sought therapy, and then joined a new training environment at University of Texas where she felt supported by coaches and teammates. Lydia learned to *notice the warning signs* in herself and "be proactive and see my therapist before it gets to a point where I'm not able to do the things I need to be doing". Her story shows that when athletes are given the right tools – education about mental health, coping strategies, openness to professional help – they can rebound from the post-competition crash. In Lydia's case, she came back to win again, and, more importantly, committed to speaking out to reduce the stigma so others won't suffer in silence.

In summary, the sports psychologist's toolbox is an invaluable complement to the athlete's support system. It provides structured, evidence-based methods to cope with the emotional rollercoaster that can follow a win (or any intense sporting experience). These professionals teach athletes that mental health is trainable and that seeking help is not a weakness but a wise strategy – just like hiring a coach for physical training. With techniques like cognitive reframing, counseling, relaxation training, group support, and identity work, athletes gain skills to handle the "hangover" after the podium. And armed with these skills, they are far better prepared to transition to the next chapter of their lives with resilience and confidence.

Building a Post-Competition Game Plan

One of the most empowering strategies to beat the post-competition crash is to plan for it in advance. Just as an athlete wouldn't step onto the field without a game plan, they shouldn't step off the podium without a plan for the days, weeks, and years afterward. In elite sports circles, there's a growing recognition that *planning for life after the big event is as essential as training for the event itself*. This means athletes and their support teams actively think about "What comes next?" even as they prepare for competition, integrating the "after" phase into the athletic journey rather than treating it as an afterthought.

Some forward-thinking sports organizations have started implementing formal programs to help athletes with this transition. For example, Olympic committees and national sports federations now offer career development and transition resources. The U.S. Olympic & Paralympic Committee has a "Life After Sport" initiative that provides resources to help athletes "take that next step towards the passions that lie ahead" in their post-competition life. This can include education programs, job networking, and career counseling made available before the athlete even leaves competition. Similarly, the International Olympic Committee developed an Athlete365 Career+ program that assists Olympians in preparing for post-sport careers – through workshops on resume building, mentorship opportunities in various industries, and even placements or internships. The idea behind these programs is clear: an athlete who has a sense of direction beyond sport is less likely to feel lost when their competitive days wind down.

But planning isn't just about careers; it's also about decompression and personal fulfillment. Many experts now advise athletes to line up *activities or interests* for immediately after a major competition – *before* the competition even happens. For instance, some Olympic teams schedule optional group vacations or retreats for athletes right after the closing ceremony, giving them a chance to unwind together away from the pressures of home media and expectations. It turns out this isn't just a nice perk, but actually research-backed: scheduling a vacation or a trip home can aid mental recovery. Knowing that a relaxing getaway or quality family time is on the calendar can also serve as a mental safety net for athletes as they compete – they know that whatever happens, there's a planned period of rest and reward.

Athletes themselves have found creative ways to ensure they don't fall into a void after the big day. Consider the story of a track cyclist who spent four years preparing for the World Championships. On the advice of her sports psychologist, a month before the event she enrolled in a short photography course that would start two weeks after the competition. Winning a medal was her dream, but she also knew she needed something else on the horizon. She did win – and in the week after, as the adrenaline dip hit her, she found herself surprisingly excited to dive into the photography class. It gave her brain a new challenge and a creative outlet at just the right time, preventing the total loss of structure that so many athletes struggle with. Another example: an Olympic weightlifter arranged to begin volunteering at a local charity shortly after the Olympics. In interviews, he said having that volunteer work – helping rebuild homes in a community – gave him perspective and a sense of purpose beyond his sport, making the post-Olympic months some of the most rewarding rather than depressing. Stories like these highlight a key point: a small non-sport goal can act like a bridge over the chasm of the post-competition period.

Planning for the "after" also involves handling the sudden change in daily routine. High-level athletes are used to highly regimented schedules. Come Monday after a big event, there's often *no practice, no meetings, no flight to catch – nothing.* That abrupt halt can be psychologically jarring. A good post-competition game plan anticipates this. Athletes are encouraged to maintain some healthy routines even during their off-time: maybe it's waking up at a reasonable hour and doing light exercise or yoga each morning, or scheduling a standing weekly hike with friends. Maintaining a bit of routine provides structure and can prevent the aimlessness that feeds anxiety and low mood. As mentioned earlier, maintaining some level of physical activity is beneficial – stopping exercise cold turkey can actually worsen mood due to the sudden withdrawal of all those endorphins. Many successful athletes intentionally taper down their training post-competition instead of quitting it outright. For example, a marathoner might switch to easy swims and walks for a few weeks – keeping the body moving but without the intensity or pressure of training. Combined with proper rest (because yes, *rest* is part of the plan too), this approach helps balance their physiology and energy levels.

There's also an identity component to the post-competition plan. Earlier in the chapter, we touched on the importance of athletes exploring roles beyond sport. A good plan encourages athletes to invest time in other aspects of their identity. This could mean reconnecting with hobbies that fell by the wayside during training. Maybe the Olympic fencer loves playing guitar but hadn't touched the instrument in months; as part of her plan, she might commit to jamming with friends every Friday night after the tournament. Or an NBA player who just won a championship might finally take that family fishing trip he's talked about for years. The goal is to *remind the athlete that they are more than their sport* — and to do so through activities that genuinely bring them joy or peace. In practice, some teams now hold workshops *before* a major event where athletes brainstorm a personal "post-event plan." They list at least one thing they will do for fun, one thing for personal growth, and one social connection to pursue after the season ends. Such exercises can be surprisingly effective. Athletes report that having even a rough sketch for the next step reduces the anxiety of the unknown. It's easier to climb down from the summit when you can see the path ahead.

Sports governing bodies are beginning to bake this into their culture. Olympic programs in certain countries have started including sessions on career planning and mental decompression before the Games conclude. During the Tokyo 2020 (held in 2021) Olympics, the USOPC's mental health team was actively encouraging athletes to utilize on-site counselors to talk not just about competition stress but about the transition afterward. Some delegations organized "life after sport" discussion panels in the Olympic village, featuring former athletes who had successfully transitioned to new careers, to inspire current competitors that there is a rich life beyond medals. The presence of these conversations right at the height of competition signals an important cultural change: acknowledging that the *after-phase exists and matters.*

Nothing illustrates the value of a post-competition plan better than hearing athletes who've lived through the crash advocate for it. Two-time Olympic gold medalist Briana Scurry often speaks to younger athletes about preparing for retirement even as they chase medals. "Ask yourself, who am I without my game?" she says – not to be discouraging, but to prompt athletes to cultivate that answer while still competing. Scurry credits the fact that she did this reflection with helping her find a new calling after soccer. She also advises Olympians to make a post-Olympics life plan with concrete steps: maybe sign up for a workshop or professional development course that starts soon after the Games, or schedule time to visit family. Little things like booking a flight home or a holiday in advance can provide a gentle landing, as research has shown such planned vacations help in emotionally transitioning away from the intensity of competition. Another retired Olympian, swimmer Kate Knifton, learned from a near career-ending injury the importance of not waiting until the end to think about the future. "Your body has a reaction from doing all this training and then suddenly doing nothing at all," she said, explaining why she's now careful to have "things in place for myself for one day…when I'm not rowing". For Knifton, that meant finishing her education and exploring internships even as she trained for Paris 2024 – moves that ensured she had more than one identity and one direction in life.

Athletes who embrace such planning often find that the "podium hangover" is milder or shorter-lived. They have something to look forward to and a roadmap for the transition. Importantly, these plans aren't rigid or one-size-fits-all. They're personal and flexible – because life, especially after sport, can be unpredictable. The aim isn't to schedule every hour post-competition, but to avoid the scenario of an athlete standing in their living room days after glory thinking, "What do I do now?" There should be at least a partial answer to that question ready.

On a structural level, sports organizations are now viewing the "after" phase as part of the athlete's journey. The creation of dedicated mental health divisions, athlete wellness programs, and career transition services (like the USOPC's Athlete Career Education program and similar ones in the UK, Australia, and Canada) all reflect this holistic approach. Athletes are increasingly supported *through* the transition, not just dropped at the finish line. This holistic care may well extend athletic careers (since athletes feel more supported) and improve life outcomes, turning champions into well-adjusted alumni who can contribute to society in new ways.

In wrapping up this chapter, the recurring theme is clear: planning and support make all the difference. The podium hangover is real, but it is not insurmountable. With a team of support – coaches who continue to mentor, family and teammates who uplift, psychologists who equip with tools, and proactive planning for the road ahead – athletes can beat the post-competition crash. They can rebuild their identity piece by piece, integrating the triumph into a larger sense of purpose. They can transition into life beyond the medal not as a fall from grace, but as a new adventure for which they are mentally trained. Every ending in sport is, after all, a beginning of something else. And with the right support systems in place, that "something else" can be just as fulfilling as standing on the podium, if not more. The true gold in an athlete's life may well be the people and plans that carry them forward when the roar of the crowd fades – the team that proves, in the end, none of us wins alone, and none of us has to heal alone.

Chapter 7

Rebuilding Identity – Crafting Life Beyond the Uniform

The competition is over, the medals are won, and the roar of the crowd has faded. In the quiet after the victory, many athletes find themselves asking one profound question: *Who am I, if I'm not defined by my sport?* This chapter tackles that question head-on. It's about rebuilding identity, embracing life beyond the uniform, and discovering that the end of an athletic career is not really an end at all – it can be the beginning of a new journey. We explore how to become a "whole person" beyond being an athlete, how to channel the same strengths that made you a champion into new passions, how to find purpose outside of competition, and how to set inspiring goals for your next chapter. Grounded in contemporary psychology and real-world stories, the tone here is both informational and motivational – a reassuring guide to carrying the flame of excellence into every arena of life after sport.

From Athlete to "Whole Person"

One of the first steps in rebuilding your identity is recognizing that you are more than your sport. For years, you may have been known solely as "the swimmer," "the basketball player," or "the gymnast." Your days were filled with training and competition, and it's understandable that stepping away from that world can leave you feeling like a piece of yourself is missing. However, sports psychologists remind us that athletes are *whole individuals*, not just competitors. You have other roles – perhaps as a friend, a student, a creator, a family member – that have always been part of you. Embracing those other facets is key to crafting a fulfilling life beyond the medal stand.

Psychological research supports the idea that expanding your identity leads to a smoother transition out of sport. Studies of retired elite athletes show that those who pursued education or hobbies alongside their athletic career adjusted better to post-sport life than those who were entirely focused on athletics. In essence, having multiple pursuits creates a safety net for your sense of self. If the athlete role changes or ends, you still have other sources of identity to draw on. Developing a "dual identity" (sports *and* non-sports self) even during your playing days can buffer the shock of retirement or an extended break. But it's **never too late** to expand your sense of self. Even now, small steps like spending time on non-sport hobbies or social activities can plant seeds for a fuller identity.

Where to begin? Consider the parts of you that might have been set aside during your athletic career. Is there a hobby or interest you once loved that got squeezed out by your training schedule? Maybe you enjoyed music, art, or writing as a kid but haven't picked that up in years. Or perhaps you always wanted to explore a subject academically or develop a professional skill beyond sports. Start *small*. For example, one former track athlete who missed the creative outlet of music began taking a weekly guitar lesson, and an Olympic gymnast enrolled in a couple of college courses after retiring. These modest steps brought each of them joy and a sense of progress completely separate from competition. The specific activity matters less than the act of reconnecting with an interest beyond the field. By reviving a childhood hobby or learning something new, you remind yourself that you have talents and sources of enjoyment that have nothing to do with winning medals.

Rebuilding your identity as a whole person also means nurturing relationships and roles outside of athletics. During your competitive years, much of your social life likely revolved around teammates and coaches. Now is the time to reconnect with family and friends whose support you may have missed, and to engage with new people who share your non-sport interests. You might join a local hiking club, a volunteer group, or take a cooking class – activities that plug you into a community where "athlete" isn't the main definition of who you are. Expanding your social circle in this way can subtly shift how you see yourself: not only as a former athlete, but as a friend, a mentor, a student, or simply a person who enjoys a variety of experiences.

This shift in identity can feel unsettling at first – like navigating without your old compass. Be patient and give yourself grace. Remember that identity is not fixed; it evolves throughout life. You are in the process of becoming something new, and that's an exciting prospect. By telling yourself "I am more than my sport" and taking action to grow those other parts of you, you're laying a strong foundation for the future. When one chapter (competitive athletics) ends, others are already in motion. Over time, as you invest in these different roles and interests, you'll start to feel the truth of that idea: you are *so much more* than what it said on the back of your jersey.

Translating Athletic Prowess into New Passions

The very qualities that made you an elite athlete can become the superpowers that propel you in your next chapter. Think of the traits you honed over years of training: discipline, resilience, teamwork, leadership, time management, and the ability to perform under pressure. These strengths did not vanish when you hung up your jersey – they are transferable skills you carry into any new pursuit. Now it's time to leverage your champion's mindset in new arenas of life, whether that's a second career, a personal project, or an entirely different passion.

Many former athletes have successfully channeled their athletic drive into other fields. For instance, an Olympic swimmer channeled her competitive energy into a fitness startup. She found that setting business goals and grinding daily to achieve them gave her a familiar thrill, akin to training for a big meet. When faced with obstacles in her company, she tackled them like she would a tough opponent in the pool – with creative problem-solving and tenacity. Similarly, a professional football player transitioned into coaching a youth team after retirement. His deep understanding of teamwork and leadership on the field made him a natural mentor. By guiding young athletes, he found a renewed sense of purpose. He was still "in the game," just in a different role, and the camaraderie and focus he brought to coaching were direct extensions of his strengths as a team captain.

Others pivot in completely new directions. Perhaps you have a hidden interest in technology, the arts, or community activism. One former track champion, for example, took his legendary work ethic into the tech sector. He attended a coding boot camp and applied the same persistence he used in training to learn software development – eventually landing a job at a tech startup. Another retired athlete discovered a love for painting and poured hours into art classes, using her eye for detail and patience (traits sharpened through sport) to create impressive artwork that she later exhibited. Some athletes turn to advocacy or social entrepreneurship, channeling their passion for excellence into making a difference beyond sport. The content of their work changed, but the *approach* remained: the drive, focus, and commitment forged in sport were redirected toward new goals.

Science backs up the idea that your brain and body are primed to excel in new pursuits. Neuroscientists have found that the brain's capacity for adaptation – its **neuroplasticity** – does not suddenly halt in adulthood. The intense mental training you went through as an athlete (mastering techniques, memorizing playbooks, staying cool under pressure) actually strengthened neural pathways that can now be used for learning entirely new skills. In plain terms, you've spent years training your brain to learn, focus, and overcome challenges. That gives you a head start when you dive into any unfamiliar endeavor. You might notice that you approach new tasks with a built-in resilience – knowing that practice leads to improvement, and being familiar with the cycle of trial, error, and eventual success. Not everyone in the general population has that mindset ingrained, but you do.

Psychologists also note that identifying and applying your athletic transferable skills can boost your confidence during this transition. You may initially feel like a novice in a new job or activity, but remember the extensive toolkit you bring. Without even realizing it, you've developed stellar communication and leadership abilities, learned how to set clear goals, and become adept at time management and self-motivation. These are exactly the qualities that employers, colleagues, and communities value. Recognizing this can be empowering. In fact, mental health professionals who work with former athletes often have their clients list the life skills gained from sport – doing so tends to replace feelings of uncertainty with a sense of capability. One former athlete put it this way: *"I realized I wasn't starting from scratch in my new career – I was starting from experience."*

The takeaway message is that your medal-winning mindset is an asset beyond sport. The thrill of pushing toward a goal and the satisfaction of achievement are not confined to arenas and stadiums; they can be found in boardrooms, classrooms, studios, or community projects. You've already proven that you can dedicate yourself to mastery and handle adversity. Now, by translating that prowess into new passions, you can find meaning and success in a whole new domain. Instead of defining yourself by what you *used* to do, you start to build confidence in what you *can do next*. In this way, leaving competitive sport isn't about losing your identity – it's about expanding it.

Pursuing Purpose: Values and Meaning Beyond Medals

During an athletic career, everything is guided by a clear purpose – a "why" – whether it's the love of the game, striving for excellence, or representing your community. So it's no surprise that when competition ends, many athletes feel adrift. It's common to experience a void and even an identity crisis, asking yourself, *What is my purpose now that I'm not competing?* This section is about discovering a new "why" in life beyond the medals.

A key insight from positive psychology is that long-term well-being comes from having a sense of meaning that aligns with your core values. In other words, know what matters most to you – whether it's helping others, creativity, learning, family, leadership, or something else – and build your next chapter around those priorities. Athletes in transition can benefit greatly from clarifying their values. Think about what truly energizes and fulfills you at a deeper level. During your sports days, your "why" might have been chasing victory or pushing your personal limits. But outside of sports, it could be anything from contributing to your community, to exploring new knowledge, to being deeply present with loved ones.

One Olympic skier, after her final Games, fell into a post-competition depression. With the competition over, she felt empty inside. In reflecting on her core values, she realized she cared deeply about nature and the environment – not surprising, given she'd spent years in the mountains training. She decided to channel that value into action: she began volunteering with an environmental conservation group. She soon found that protecting the outdoors gave her a similar spark to racing. She even went on to earn a degree in environmental policy, joking that she went from winning gold medals to planting trees. By pursuing a cause tied to her love of nature, she discovered a fresh purpose that made her excited to get up in the morning.

Another former athlete, a professional basketball player, realized that one of his deepest values was helping others. After retiring, he started a youth mentorship program in his hometown, using basketball as a tool to teach life skills. Guiding disadvantaged kids and seeing them grow gave him a profound sense of fulfillment. He even described one young person's success as *"the most meaningful win of my life."* By focusing on uplifting others, he built a purpose outside of sports that brought him pride and motivation each day.

Your own purpose might spring from similar reflections. What do you want your life to stand for beyond athletics? Some athletes find purpose in giving back to their sport (like coaching, mentorship, or activism), others in entirely new areas. Perhaps you value education – maybe you'll finish that degree you postponed or become a teacher. If you value creativity, you might write a book, launch a business, or take up painting. If community matters to you, you could get involved in local charities or social causes that inspire you. There's no right or wrong answer; what matters is that it resonates with you personally. One useful exercise is to list your top values and brainstorm a way to honor each of them in this new chapter. For example, if *leadership* is a core value, you might take on a project at work or coach a local team. If *creativity* is key, you could start that blog or art class you've been dreaming about.

By living your values, you redefine your identity in an authentic and resilient way. When your purpose is tied to something fundamental (like helping others, learning, or creativity), it isn't as fragile as the win–loss record of a season. In your athletic days, a serious injury or a big loss could shake your sense of self-worth, because so much was pinned on that one role. But now, if one pursuit doesn't work out or changes, you have a broader foundation to stand on. You are not defined solely by the title of athlete – you are someone who stands for your values, and there are many ways to live those out. This makes your post-sport identity more adaptable to life's ups and downs.

Many retired athletes come to find that life after sport can be deeply rewarding once they identify a purpose that truly matters to them. It may take some searching, but remember: your life's meaning was never limited to medals and championships. By following what truly matters to you, you'll build an identity – and a life – that feels genuinely worthwhile long after the final whistle.

Goals for the Next Chapter

Elite athletes excel at setting goals and pursuing them with dedication. That approach can be just as powerful after sports. Think of life after competition as a new season – a different playing field, but the same winning mindset. It's not a free fall; it's simply the next event to train for. Just as you once mapped out a training schedule or season plan, now you can map out objectives for this next phase of life. Consider setting both short-term and long-term goals. In the short term, you might aim to complete a professional course or pick up a new hobby over the next few months. Long-term goals could include finishing a degree in the next few years, starting a business or family, or even training for an adventure like a marathon.

When setting these goals, don't forget the techniques that served you well in sports. One classic approach is to ensure your goals are S.M.A.R.T.: Specific, Measurable, Achievable, Relevant, and Time-bound. For instance, instead of a fuzzy goal like "I want a new career," you could specify: "I will complete an online certification in sports management by the end of this year and then apply to several jobs in that field." That goal checks all the SMART boxes – it's concrete and has a timeline, so you can track progress. Similarly, use the power of visualization as you did in sport: picture yourself achieving your new goals, whether it's acing a job interview, walking across a stage to receive a diploma, or simply feeling healthy and purposeful in your daily routine. Mental rehearsal can boost your confidence and keep you focused, just as imagining a perfect performance used to psych you up before a game.

Break big goals into smaller steps, just like a tough training regimen. For example, if your long-term goal is to start a business, outline phases: idea and research, seeking a mentor, securing funding, and so on. Each step completed gives you a sense of accomplishment and momentum – much like hitting personal bests in training.

It can also help to learn from peers who have navigated this transition. One Olympian even created a "retirement training plan." She jotted down immediate goals (such as reconnecting with friends and trying internships in two new fields within a year) and longer-term goals (like finishing her degree in four years and finding a career she loves). She approached it like a workout schedule – checking her progress regularly and adjusting as needed. With that roadmap, she never felt aimless.

In setting new ambitions, include goals that nurture you as a person, not just as a professional. Maybe you want to travel to places you've always dreamed of or dedicate time each week to a hobby or to family. These personal goals are just as important as career goals – they keep your life balanced and enjoyable.

Also, remember to pace yourself. The same drive that made you a champion could tempt you to push too hard now, but progress takes time – you don't have to "win" life after sport overnight. Just as you built in rest during training, allow yourself time to adjust and grow at a sustainable pace. There may be setbacks or dips in motivation – that's normal. When those happen, recall how you pushed through slumps in training and kept going. You know how to persevere.

Conclusion: Reaching the podium was a great triumph, but it was never meant to be your final destination – just one milestone among many. Now you have the opportunity to carry the same passion and commitment into new endeavors. Remember, your identity is not a fixed label handed to you by medals or headlines; it's an evolving story, and you hold the pen. With every new goal you set and every value-driven choice you make, you are crafting the next chapters of who you are. Embrace the process with the heart of a competitor and the curiosity of a beginner. Life beyond the uniform is a new arena, but you're equipped to thrive. The next victory, in whatever form, awaits – and you have everything you need to achieve it.

Chapter 8

Training the Mind for Life – Applying Performance Psychology Beyond Sport

Life beyond the finish line presents a new kind of arena for elite athletes. After years of regimented training and intense competition, the challenge becomes navigating everyday life without the familiar structure of sport. Training the mind for life means applying those same performance psychology principles that fueled athletic success to one's post-competition well-being. In this chapter, we explore how mental skills honed in sport—mindfulness, growth mindset, emotional coping strategies, and even neuroscience-backed insights—can empower former champions to thrive beyond the medal podium. The tone blends grounded scientific insight with motivational inspiration, showing that the end of an athletic career is not a decline but a transformation. Just as muscles are kept strong through exercise, the mind can be trained and strengthened for life's next chapter.

Mindfulness and Mental Resilience

Many elite athletes have long credited mindfulness practices—such as meditation, controlled breathing, and visualization—for giving them a mental edge in competition. These techniques sharpened their focus before big games and helped manage performance anxiety. Now, beyond sport, those same practices become vital tools for post-competition resilience. Mindfulness is essentially the art of paying attention to the present moment without judgment. By sitting quietly with one's thoughts or focusing on the rhythm of breath, a retired athlete can learn to *observe* waves of worry or sadness without being swept away by them. Research shows that meditation is a proven method to reduce stress and anxiety while also boosting mood and cognitive function. In practical terms, ten minutes of mindful breathing in the morning might replace the ten minutes of pre-game visualization they used to do; this simple habit can lower daily stress hormones and promote calm clarity.

Let's consider a real-world example of how mindfulness can be life-changing after sports. *One former NFL player*, forced into retirement by injury, spiraled into a dark depression where he nearly lost all sense of purpose. In an interview, he revealed that meditation literally saved his life, giving him a way to cope with pain and loss when football was suddenly gone. This athlete described sitting in silence each day, learning to "be with himself" and confront difficult emotions instead of running from them. Over time, this mindfulness practice lifted him from his darkest moment. What began as a tool to mentally reset during injury rehab ultimately became a lifelong habit for handling stress in retirement. His story illustrates how the same mindful attention that helped him focus on the field could also help him heal and find peace off the field.

Beyond anecdotes, science backs the power of mindfulness for those in transition. Mindfulness-based programs have been found especially effective for retired athletes, with older athletes seeing major mental health benefits from these practices. Part of the reason is that mindfulness trains the brain's capacity to regulate emotion. Studies in neuroscience show that mindfulness meditation can literally change the brain: long-term meditators exhibit improved emotional regulation and even structural changes in brain regions linked to stress and attention. Put simply, mindfulness strengthens the "mental muscle" that keeps a person grounded and resilient. For someone no longer living by strict training schedules, practicing mindfulness creates a new kind of inner routine. It anchors them when feelings of anxiety or aimlessness arise in the more open, unstructured days of retirement.

Moreover, mindfulness techniques that were *staples of high-performance psychology*—like guided imagery and deep breathing—remain just as useful after the medals are won. Many athletes are familiar with using visualization to rehearse a perfect race or taking slow breaths to calm pre-competition nerves. In retirement, these techniques can be repurposed to quell panic during a stressful work presentation or to find calm when one's mind races with "What now?" thoughts. Psychologists note that mindfulness meditation changes our brain and biology in positive ways, improving mental health. By embracing mindfulness, former competitors train their attention and awareness, building the same kind of mental resilience for life's ups and downs that they once built for sports. An Olympian who once centered herself in the seconds before the starting gun can use those exact skills to center herself before a job interview or when coping with an injury in daily life. In this way, mindfulness becomes a bridge between the structured world of elite sport and the wider, unpredictable world beyond it—keeping athletes grounded, focused, and resilient no matter what comes next.

The Growth Mindset in Transition

Another key to thriving after the cheering stops is adopting a growth mindset about the future. Pioneered by psychologist Carol Dweck, the growth mindset is the belief that abilities and intelligence can be developed through effort, good strategies, and input from others. In sports, champions often demonstrate this mindset by treating each challenge or loss as fuel to improve rather than as a verdict on their talent. Now, in the transition to normal life, a growth mindset can make the difference between feeling like one's best days are over and feeling excited to learn new things. Dweck herself noted that a growth mindset allows athletes to "embrace learning [and] welcome challenges, mistakes, and feedback". This attitude is crucial when athletes find themselves as novices again in new careers or hobbies.

Imagine a retired Olympian who decides to take up a completely new profession, say marketing or coding. Initially, she might feel frustrated – she went from being world-class in her sport to feeling clumsy at basic office tasks. It's tempting for her to think, "I'm just not cut out for this," a trace of the fixed mindset (which assumes abilities are static). But if she recalls how she approached training as an athlete, she'll remember that mastery came through being *open to growth*: breaking big goals into small steps, learning from errors, and steadily gaining skill. With a growth mindset, she reframes the situation: "This new job is hard because it's new, but I can improve with time and effort." She gives herself permission to be a beginner. By viewing the post-sport phase as a chance to grow rather than a decline, she mirrors the same mentality that drove her athletic progress. Psychologists emphasize that how one engages with challenges – seeing them as opportunities rather than threats – will influence future behavior and success. In other words, the self-belief that "I can adapt and learn" becomes a self-fulfilling prophecy for a fulfilling second act.

Cultivating a growth mindset during this transition involves practical steps. Curiosity is one: staying open-minded and asking questions in unfamiliar domains instead of fearing looking ignorant. Embracing effort is another: just as an athlete once embraced grueling practice sessions, now they can embrace the effort of studying for a certification or practicing a new skill. It also requires patience and self-compassion. A former competitor who was used to excelling might struggle with the ego hit of starting from scratch. In those moments, remembering that every champion was once a novice helps. The same perseverance that led to improvement in sport can be redirected to, say, learning to play guitar or pursuing a business degree. A growth mindset guides one's response to setbacks, fostering self-reflection and adaptation rather than defeatism. For example, if a new hobby doesn't come naturally at first, instead of thinking "I'm too old to learn this," a growth-minded individual will think "This is tough now, which means I'm pushing my boundaries and my brain is forming new connections. What can I try differently next time?"

The benefits of a growth mindset are not just philosophical; they're grounded in research. Studies have shown that people with a growth mindset cope better with change and maintain higher motivation and well-being compared to those with a fixed mindset. In sports psychology, growth mindset is linked to greater resilience – athletes high in this trait tend to bounce back from losses faster and continue to seek improvement. Crucially, these same traits help in life beyond sport. When an athlete views the post-retirement phase as *another arena to excel in*, they are more likely to find purpose and satisfaction. In fact, neuroscience research suggests that adopting a growth mindset engages brain pathways associated with intrinsic motivation and learning, and these neural connections can be "repurposed" for challenges outside of sport. In essence, the brain that learned to adapt to a new play or opponent is well-equipped to adapt to a new office environment or life role. By consciously choosing a growth mindset, former athletes set themselves up to keep growing, keep learning, and keep finding victories long after the final whistle of their sports career.

Emotional Fitness and Coping Skills

Throughout their careers, elite athletes invest countless hours in physical training to stay in peak condition. In retirement, there's an equally important regimen to follow: emotional fitness. Just as one would schedule regular workouts to maintain physical strength, it's vital to schedule and practice mental and emotional exercises to maintain psychological well-being. This section presents a toolkit of evidence-based coping skills—many borrowed from sports psychology and cognitive-behavioral therapy (CBT)—that can help manage emotions and stress. Think of it as a personalized training program for your mental health, where skills like self-talk, visualization, and stress management are your "exercises," and consistency is key to seeing results. By treating mental health proactively, former athletes can build resilience day by day, much as they once built endurance or muscle in the gym.

1. Positive Self-Talk: The way we speak to ourselves has a powerful impact on mood and confidence. Athletes often use self-talk strategically: a sprinter might repeat a mantra like "strong and fast" before a race, or a weightlifter might psych themselves up with "I've got this, one rep at a time." This internal dialogue can be harnessed in everyday life too. For instance, before a challenging presentation at work, giving yourself a silent pep talk ("I am prepared and capable") can steady your nerves. Research indicates that positive self-talk boosts self-confidence and reduces anxiety, which in turn improves performance. In the context of life beyond sport, performance might mean anything from acing an interview to simply getting through a tough day. By deliberately choosing encouraging, constructive thoughts, you coach yourself through challenges. It can be as simple as countering a negative thought ("I can't handle this") with a positive reframe ("I will handle this, just like I've handled pressure before"). Over time, these affirmations become mental habits, providing an *on-demand* morale boost when you need it most. Importantly, self-talk isn't about blind cheerleading; it's about realistic optimism – reminding yourself of your strengths and focusing on solutions. Elite performers from Michael Jordan to Olympic swimmers have used self-talk to stay focused and resilient under pressure, and those same techniques can help anyone persist through a long meeting or cope with a personal setback.

2. Visualization and Imagery: In sports, mental imagery is a staple of training. Athletes vividly *visualize* executing the perfect routine or scoring the game-winning point. This practice doesn't stop at retirement's door. Visualization can be repurposed as a coping skill for future goals and daily stresses. For example, if a former gymnast is nervous about a public speaking event, she can close her eyes beforehand and imagine herself walking confidently on stage, delivering a successful speech, and feeling the gratification afterward. This mental dress rehearsal primes the brain for the real experience. In fact, scientists have found that visualizing an action activates many of the same neural pathways as physically performing it, strengthening those connections and even enhancing muscle memory. In essence, when you repeatedly imagine yourself handling a situation well, you're training your brain to make it so. Visualization also helps with emotional resilience: one can mentally play out potential challenges (like an interview question you dread or a difficult conversation with a family member) and see oneself coping calmly. Sports psychologists note that visualizing both positive outcomes *and* tough scenarios improves adaptability – "rehearsing" adversity in your mind builds confidence that you can face it for real. There's even evidence that guided imagery can spur physiological changes: some research suggests that entering a relaxed, focused imagery state can alter brain wave patterns and stress biochemistry, leading to faster healing and reduced anxiety. For the retired athlete, visualization is like keeping an internal playbook for life – a way to continue using the power of mental rehearsal to achieve personal victories and remain poised under pressure.

3. Stress Inoculation: High-level competitors are no strangers to stress; what sets them apart is their conditioned response to it. One advanced technique used in both therapy and sport psychology is *Stress Inoculation Training (SIT)*. The concept is akin to a vaccine: by exposing oneself to small, manageable doses of stress, you build immunity against larger stresses. In practice, this might involve deliberately practicing coping skills under simulated pressure. For instance, a former athlete might purposefully engage in challenging situations—taking a difficult class, competing in a low-stakes local tournament of a new sport, or even public speaking at a community event—to practice managing nerves and emotions. Each controlled exposure is an opportunity to apply relaxation techniques, positive self-talk, and problem-solving in real time. Over time, those skills get stronger, and anxiety about the "real" tough events diminishes. Clinical evidence shows that stress inoculation can improve performance in high-pressure situations by enhancing coping skills and emotional regulation. By gradually raising the threshold of what you can handle, you develop a hardy resilience. For example, if the idea of job interviews causes intense anxiety, one could start by practicing with a friend acting as the interviewer (a mild stressor), then progress to informational interviews or mock interviews with strangers, before facing an actual high-stakes interview. At each step, you'd practice calming your breathing and reframing negative thoughts, so your confidence grows alongside the challenge. This method, rooted in cognitive-behavioral therapy, has been used to train soldiers and surgeons to perform under pressure. Athletes, too, have used it (sometimes unknowingly) when coaches simulate loud crowd noise or tricky race conditions in practice to "inoculate" them against those stressors. In everyday life, think of stress inoculation as *fitness training for your nervous system* – push it just enough, recover, and watch your capacity expand.

4. Proactive Recovery and Routine: Emotional fitness isn't only about pushing yourself; it's also about recovery and maintenance. Athletes know the importance of cool-downs and rest days for their bodies – the same applies to the mind. Incorporating regular recovery practices like journaling, therapy sessions, or relaxation exercises can keep mental health strong. Journaling, for example, is a simple habit with big benefits. Writing down one's thoughts and feelings provides an outlet to process emotions and reflect on challenges. Many Olympians have used journaling to sharpen focus, set goals, and manage stress during their careers, and they carry this habit into retirement. By putting worries or plans on paper, you organize your mind and often gain perspective on what you're feeling. One might journal each evening as a way to "cool down" the mind—acknowledging any anxieties and recording small wins of the day. This practice has been shown to support emotional resilience by preventing rumination and helping individuals maintain balance.

Likewise, seeking professional support such as therapy or counseling can be framed as mental cross-training. In the same way a marathoner might add cycling or yoga to enhance her physical conditioning, a former athlete can use therapy as a complementary workout for the mind. There is no shame in this; on the contrary, it's a sign of strength and dedication to self-improvement. Michael Phelps, the most decorated Olympian, has openly stated that therapy "saved my life" during his post-Olympic depression. He treated his mental health with the same seriousness as his physical health, continuing therapy after rehab and learning tools to manage his emotions day-to-day. Many other athletes have echoed that sentiment, urging peers to get help when needed. By scheduling regular therapy sessions or mental health check-ins, you ensure that you're not just reacting to problems after they become overwhelming, but actively building coping strategies and emotional awareness. Think of a weekly therapy appointment or support group as you would think of a weekly team practice – a non-negotiable part of your routine that keeps you in shape. Even activities like meditation or yoga, when done consistently, act as preventative maintenance for the psyche, much like stretching and nutrition keep the body tuned.

In summary, approaching mental health proactively means treating it as an ongoing training process. You wouldn't expect to stay physically strong if you stopped training for months; similarly, emotional strength can dwindle without upkeep. The encouraging news is that even small, regular practices compound over time. A retired marathoner who dedicates 15 minutes each morning to mindfulness and 30 minutes each week to a therapy session may find that she handles daily stresses with the same poise and endurance that she once brought to the racecourse. By viewing journaling, meditation, self-talk, and other techniques as emotional fitness routines, former athletes maintain a sense of discipline and purpose. They channel the same drive that once aimed at breaking records into the new goal of sustaining mental wellness. The result is not only a smoother transition out of sport but also a richer, more balanced life in the years that follow.

Neuroscience of Reinvention

One of the most inspiring revelations of modern neuroscience is that the human brain can change and adapt at any age. This concept, known as neuroplasticity, offers a powerful message for anyone leaving a long sports career: it's *never* too late to reinvent yourself. The same brain that learned the intricate skills of a sport through years of practice is fully capable of learning the rhythms of a new lifestyle or vocation. In this section, we bridge cutting-edge science with the athlete's journey of reinvention, showing that change is not only possible – it is biologically built-in. The tone here is optimistic and scientific, reinforcing that just as muscles grow stronger with training, the brain can grow and rewire itself when challenged with new learning.

To understand the neuroscience of reinvention, consider what happens in the brain when we acquire a new skill. Each repetition of a task—be it a tennis serve or a piano scale—strengthens specific neural pathways. Neurons that fire together wire together, as the saying goes, meaning the brain's circuits literally reorganize to become more efficient at whatever is repeatedly practiced. This is how an athlete's brain adapted over years to optimize coordination, reflexes, and decision-making for their sport. Now, when entering a new chapter of life, those well-honed circuits may not be in constant use, but the brain's capacity to form *new* circuits remains. Emerging research shows that neuroplasticity allows the brain to retain an incredible ability to adapt structurally and functionally throughout life. Even though certain cognitive abilities might slow slightly with age, the fundamental ability to learn and change does not vanish. In fact, scientists have found that older adults who engage in novel learning activities (like picking up a new language or hobby) can spur significant brain changes and improvements in cognitive function. The key is engagement: much like a muscle, the brain thrives on "exercise."

One vivid example of neuroplasticity's power is evidence from memory research. In a landmark study, older adults who started a routine of aerobic exercise saw an actual increase in the size of their hippocampus (the brain's memory center), effectively reversing age-related volume loss and improving memory performance. This finding is stunning: it's as if a master sprinter at 65 could literally grow new muscle fibers after starting a training program. Likewise, when a retired athlete challenges their brain with new learning—be it academic coursework, learning to cook gourmet meals, or mastering chess—they are creating new neural pathways and strengthening their cognitive reserve. Neuroplasticity means the brain is malleable; it responds to our experiences and efforts. So, an athlete who fears it's "too late" to start over can take heart in knowing that their brain remains a dynamic, learning machine.

The science goes further to explain *how* this adaptation happens. When we engage in novel or complex activities, the brain increases production of neurotrophic factors (like BDNF – brain-derived neurotrophic factor) which act like fertilizer for neurons, encouraging the growth of new connections. Physical exercise is a prime example of an activity that boosts these brain growth factors. According to systematic reviews, regular physical exercise increases neuroplasticity by elevating neurotrophic factors and even promoting new cell growth, leading to better learning and memory. This is encouraging for retired athletes: by staying physically active, they not only maintain their body but also keep their brain primed for adaptation. It's no wonder that many ex-athletes report feeling mentally sharper and more emotionally balanced when they stick to a workout routine, even if it's gentler than their competitive days. Exercise, mental challenges, social engagement – all these are signals to the brain to keep remodeling and updating itself.

Neuroscientists often use the phrase "use it or lose it" when talking about the aging brain. For a former athlete, *using it* can take many forms: coaching others (which challenges the brain to explain and break down skills), pursuing education, engaging in creative hobbies, or even doing daily crossword puzzles. Each of these activities is like sending your brain to the gym. Over time, they can build cognitive resilience, sometimes called *cognitive reserve*, which is the brain's ability to cope with challenges and resist decline. Studies of retired athletes who remain mentally and physically active indicate they tend to have better cognitive health and mood compared to those who withdraw and become sedentary. In essence, staying engaged with life keeps the mind robust.

It's also worth noting the encouraging research on neuroplasticity in recovery from setbacks. The brain's adaptability is what allows stroke survivors to relearn walking or speaking; it's what allows someone to overcome trauma by forming new, healthier thought patterns. For an athlete, leaving competitive sport can feel like a kind of psychic injury—a loss of identity that the brain has to recover from. But the principle remains: through new experiences and deliberate practice, the mind heals and finds new ways of being. One might even argue that athletes are *uniquely equipped* for neuroplastic reinvention. After all, they spent years practicing constant improvement and adjustment. They know how to break a complex skill into parts and drill it until it's second nature. Now, their task is to apply that approach to something entirely different, trusting that the same process that once wired their brain for victory can now wire it for a second career or a fulfilling personal life.

In sum, the neuroscience of reinvention tells us that growth is a lifelong potential. The brain is not a static organ that peaks in one's 20s and then simply declines; it is an ever-changing network that responds to how we use it. So, for the athlete staring at the vast plain of life after sport, the message is profoundly hopeful: *you can train for this, too.* Just as you trained your body and mind for competition, you can train your brain to master new skills, adapt to new routines, and discover new passions. Every challenge you embrace – whether physical, intellectual, or emotional – sends a signal to your neurons to get to work, forge new connections, and grow. Reinvention, then, is not only a poetic concept but a biological reality. Armed with this knowledge, the retired athlete can approach the future not with fear of decline, but with the same determination and curiosity that defined their athletic rise. The podium was one pinnacle, but life has many stages—and with a resilient mind, each stage can be a platform for new achievement and meaning.

In closing, "Training the Mind for Life" means recognizing that the end of competitive sport is not the end of growth. It's a shift of arena:

from stadiums and courts to the wider world of personal and professional life. The tools of mindfulness, growth mindset, emotional fitness routines, and neuroplastic understanding form a powerful toolkit for this journey. Grounded in scientific evidence and enriched by real examples, these approaches show that *life beyond the medal* can be rich, challenging, and rewarding. With attention and practice, any former athlete can beat the post-competition crash, rebuild their identity, and indeed train for a life of purpose and fulfillment beyond the podium. The race may be different, but the finish line—healthy, holistic success—is still very much worth striving for, and it's entirely within reach.

Chapter 9

Life After Medal – Thriving in the Next Act

The roar of the crowd has faded and the medal gleams from its display case – now what? For an elite athlete, the moment after the podium can feel like standing at a crossroads. Many champions finish their sports careers in their 20s or 30s, with decades of life still ahead of them. It's a *pivotal transition*, filled with uncertainty but also rich with opportunity. This chapter explores how athletes can navigate life after the medal: building new careers, finding purpose in mentorship, redefining their relationship with health, and crafting a legacy that goes far beyond records and trophies. Grounded in real-world examples and scientific insights, the journey ahead is framed not as an ending, but as the *next act* – one where former athletes can continue to thrive with the same passion and resilience that fueled their athletic glory.

Career Crossroads and New Beginnings

At the height of competition, an athlete's path is clearly mapped out: rigorous training schedules, competition calendars, and singular goals like winning championships or Olympic medals. But when the final whistle blows or the last race is run, many athletes find themselves at a *career crossroads*. Elite sports careers are notoriously short – in major professional leagues the average retirement age hovers around the late

20s. For Olympians and athletes in individual sports, peak performance often comes in the twenties, meaning retirement can arrive startlingly early. Finishing a sports career while peers are just climbing the traditional career ladder can leave an athlete with a daunting question: What comes next?

The first part of answering that question is recognizing that *the end of sport is not the end of success, but a pivot point to new opportunities*. While nearly half of former athletes report struggling to find purpose after retiring, just as many are able to *thrive* by channeling their drive into new endeavors. It's normal to feel a sense of loss or confusion – psychologists even have a term for the identity crisis that can occur, calling it "identity foreclosure," a phenomenon likened to losing a loved one. But as challenging as this transition is, it also opens the door to reinvent oneself beyond the arena.

Navigating career transitions starts with exploring interests and education that may have been deferred for sport. Many athletes return to school or pursue higher education once their competitive days are over. Picture a champion swimmer enrolling in university classes she postponed, sitting in lectures with students years younger, diligently taking notes. In doing so, she discovers *a new passion for learning* and perhaps the seeds of a future profession. Education can provide structure and a clear goal – something athletes are accustomed to – while also expanding an athlete's identity beyond sport. In one case, an Olympian who had long dreamed of medicine traded the pool for the library, eventually completing medical school and donning a doctor's white coat.

Her discipline and endurance honed in training translated into excelling in long nights of study and hospital rotations.

Beyond formal education, *trying out different fields* through internships or mentorship programs can be invaluable. Some sports organizations and companies have started initiatives specifically for athlete transitions. For example, executives at a global firm like EY recognized that former Olympians bring distinct skills – adaptability, resilience, self-motivation – that make them valuable in the workplace. Under their athlete transition program, elite athletes are offered six-month internships with career coaching and interview training to help them shift from the locker room to the boardroom. Such programs allow athletes to test the waters in business, finance, media, or other industries, while receiving guidance in corporate culture. A retired track star might spend a summer interning at a marketing agency, discovering a knack for creative teamwork, or a former soccer player might shadow executives at a sports apparel company, learning the ropes of management. These experiences build confidence that skills from sport *are* transferrable and valued outside of it.

Indeed, career coaches who work with former athletes emphasize translating the athlete's unique background into language employers understand. Writing a résumé after years of living one's sport can be intimidating – how do you summarize "Olympic gold medalist" in a way that matters to a hiring manager? The key is to leverage those leadership, teamwork, and discipline skills that were forged in competition. Employers consistently rank teamwork, communication, and leadership among the top attributes they seek in new hires, and few people have lived those values as fully as high-level athletes. An Olympic team captain, for instance, has spent years practicing cooperation and motivating teammates under intense pressure – experiences that speak to exceptional team-building ability in any workplace. Similarly, the discipline of daily 5 A.M. training sessions or the resilience to come back from defeat are not just sports stories; they are concrete evidence of a work ethic and grit that can benefit any organization. As one career advisor puts it, former athletes haven't just learned these skills in theory – they've *embodied* them, making student-athletes and pros alike a "rare commodity" in the talent pool.

For a practical example, consider how an "athlete background" can shine in a new career: One former professional athlete applying for a business role framed his sports experience as managing high-stakes projects (games) with a diverse team, under fixed deadlines, while constantly analyzing performance metrics. He highlighted competitive achievements to demonstrate goal-setting and improvement, and noted the countless hours of practice as proof of perseverance and coachability. In interviews, he spoke about overcoming a career-threatening injury – translating it to lessons in adaptability and stress management. By shifting the perspective from "I was a football player" to "I have expertise in teamwork, performance optimization, and handling pressure," he convinced employers that *an Olympic gold or a championship ring isn't just an accolade – it's evidence of skills and character traits their company needs.*

Of course, even with the best preparation, stepping into a completely new field can be unnerving. It's akin to being a rookie all over again, except this time in the corporate office or academic classroom. There may be moments of doubt – like when a decorated athlete finds herself editing her résumé for the tenth time, wondering if years of training will ever make sense on paper. But those who have successfully transitioned remind their peers that *everyone starts somewhere.* One Olympic medalist-turned-business executive candidly shared that at first she felt behind peers her age who had a decade of industry experience. Yet, she soon realized her sports career gave her a different kind of experience – a high-performance mindset – that helped her catch up quickly. The practical tip from career transition experts and athlete programs is to seek out mentors and continue to be coachable. Just as in sport, in a new career a good mentor or coach can provide feedback and accelerate learning. Many athletes find that after the initial learning curve, they begin to *excel in their second act* with the same determination that fueled their first.

Success stories abound of athletes who found rewarding new beginnings. An Olympian from one of the most demanding sports took the plunge into medical school after retirement – trading her track spikes for textbooks – and eventually became a physician . The focus and endurance that carried her through Olympic training now benefit her patients in long hospital shifts. Another former gold medalist ended up in front of the camera as a media professional, bringing insightful commentary and charisma to sports broadcasting. Yet another channeled his competitive fire into entrepreneurship: starting a tech company and growing it with the leadership skills learned on the field. These stories illustrate that life after medal can take many forms – from medicine to media to business – and each athlete can find a path that sparks joy and fulfillment. The practical challenges (like explaining a non-traditional résumé or starting at the bottom in a new field) are real, but surmountable. With planning, support, and the *transferrable strengths* forged in sport, a retired athlete can pivot to a career that matches their interests and brings a fresh sense of achievement. In truth, leaving sport is not leaving success behind; it's carrying the best parts of it forward into new arenas.

From Medalist to Mentor – Giving Back

After years in the limelight, some athletes discover that their greatest fulfillment in retirement comes not from personal accolades, but from *uplifting others*. Moving from medalist to mentor can imbue a second act with profound meaning. Instead of chasing records, these individuals channel their passion and hard-won wisdom into service – coaching, teaching, or advocacy – effectively giving back to the community that once cheered them on. This section highlights how altruism and mentorship not only help the next generation, but also heal and inspire the champions who engage in it.

One powerful example is the champion who found purpose by returning to the fundamentals and *working with youth*. Imagine a decorated Olympian quietly opening a small sports academy in her hometown. In the same training halls where she once prepared for world competitions, now you'll find her teaching children how to do their first cartwheel or swim their first lap. This athlete-turned-coach draws on her vast experience – not to produce future Olympians per se, but to impart values of discipline, teamwork, and fun. The joy she sees in young faces when they master a new skill is as rewarding to her as any medal ceremony. In nurturing the next generation, she keeps her love for the sport alive in a new, generous way. Many real-world athletes have taken this route: former stars setting up youth academies, community sports programs, or summer camps aimed at giving kids access to sports and positive role models. Their *legacy* becomes the lives they touch. A once world-famous competitor can thus become a beloved local mentor, known not just for victory laps but for the after-school practices and encouragement they give to children.

Other athletes turn their personal struggles into a mission to help others. Consider a scenario where an Olympic swimmer who battled depression and anxiety during her career steps forward to speak out about mental health. After achieving the highest honors in her sport, she faced a *dark period* – a "post-Olympic blues" that left her feeling adrift and alone. Rather than hiding this struggle, she decides to share it publicly to break the stigma for others. One week after losing a cousin to suicide, this athlete began speaking openly about her own depression, determined to "save the next person who was struggling" by raising awareness. She partnered with a former teammate to advocate for mental health resources in sports, appearing at schools and conferences to tell her story. Over time, this shift from athlete to advocate gave her a renewed sense of purpose. The very act of helping others became therapeutic – each time she reached a young athlete who felt understood or persuaded a sports organization to prioritize mental wellness, she felt a *victory* beyond the pool. Her identity expanded from "gold medalist" to "champion for change." This is inspired by real cases (such as an Olympic swimmer who now works alongside her famous teammate to promote mental health initiatives), and it underlines a key insight: altruism can be a powerful antidote to the aimlessness that some athletes feel post-retirement. In fact, research shows that acts of altruism benefit not only the recipients but also the giver, boosting happiness and life satisfaction for the person helping. By finding *joy in helping others*, retired athletes often restore their own sense of direction and worth.

Giving back can take many forms. Some athletes stay connected to their sport through coaching at various levels – from volunteering at a local high school to taking up professional coaching roles. Others become personal trainers or sports psychologists, using their experience to guide people through fitness and mindset challenges. There are also those who move into *public speaking*, sharing lessons of perseverance, goal-setting, and resilience with audiences ranging from business leaders to youth groups. A former champion might stand on a different kind of stage now – not the Olympic podium, but an auditorium podium – delivering motivational talks that draw from the triumphs and failures of her athletic journey. In doing so, she finds that her voice is as valuable as her physical prowess once was, inspiring countless others.

Athletes who struggled in their careers sometimes find purpose by ensuring others don't face the same hurdles alone. For example, a retired athlete who once grappled with identity loss and depression might volunteer with organizations supporting transitioning athletes or even cofound a support group. They become the empathetic mentor they wished they had. One notable trend is the rise of athlete-driven foundations focusing on social causes: sports stars establishing charities for everything from education scholarships to health awareness campaigns. A former world champion might create a foundation to bring sports opportunities to underprivileged kids, remembering how access to a community center gym changed his own life trajectory. In retirement, *serving a cause* can fill the void that competition once occupied, providing structure, community, and a deep sense of purpose.

From a psychological perspective, this shift from focusing on the self (and one's performance) to focusing on others is often healing. Studies in positive psychology underscore that altruism and volunteering can reduce feelings of isolation and improve one's own mental well-being. Face-to-face helping activities, such as coaching youth or volunteering at events, create social connections and a sense of belonging that many retired athletes crave after leaving the camaraderie of their teams. In essence, *helping others helps the helper.* Brain research even suggests that altruistic acts activate reward centers and can diminish stress and pain for the giver. For an athlete who has lived a life of intense physical strain and pressure, the emotional reward of giving back can be profoundly revitalizing. One retired football player put it simply: when he started mentoring veterans and younger players, "it gave me back the drive to get out of bed in the morning," replacing the void of no longer having practice or games to attend.

For readers considering their own second act, becoming a mentor or finding a way to give back can be a win-win. It might mean coaching a little league team, sharing your expertise as a consultant, or just being available to younger athletes who seek advice. You don't have to be a famous Olympian to make a difference in someone's life; sometimes just listening to a high school athlete's worries or guiding a college player through career choices can have a lasting impact. In giving back, many former competitors discover a *rewarding second act that validates both their sports legacy and their personal growth.* They prove that their experience – the victories, the defeats, the struggles – was not only about personal glory, but also about gaining the tools to uplift others. The psychological lift of altruism restores a sense of connection and importance that can fade when the spotlight moves on. By turning the page from medalist to mentor, athletes reinforce that their story isn't over – it's entering a chapter where significance is measured not in seconds or points, but in lives touched and communities strengthened.

Lifelong Fitness and Health

Retiring from elite sport often brings a dramatic change in an athlete's relationship with physical activity and their own body. After years of regimented training schedules, strict diets, and pushing the body to its limits, stepping back can feel both liberating and unsettling. Some former athletes wake up on that first day of retirement and feel strange without the familiar ache of yesterday's workout or the urgency of today's practice. Adjusting to a new fitness routine and caring for one's long-term health becomes a crucial task in life after the medal. This section discusses how athletes can redefine exercise and health not as a relentless pursuit of perfection, but as a lifelong ally for well-being.

One common challenge is the sudden drop in training intensity. A professional or Olympic athlete might go from training 30 hours a week to essentially being "off the clock." Initially, this rest may feel like a well-earned vacation for the body. But soon, many athletes report feeling *restless or even guilty* for not maintaining the extreme regimen they're used to. There's also the physical reality that without intense training, the body will change. Weight might increase, muscle definition might soften, and endurance might decrease – all normal adjustments, yet often jarring for someone used to being in peak condition. It's not unusual for retired competitors to struggle with body image during this transition. In fact, surveys of former athletes have found that they often face issues like weight fluctuations, lingering injuries, and even body dysmorphia as they adapt to a life outside of the intense sports spotlight. Years of seeing oneself as an finely-tuned "athletic machine" can make it hard to accept a more relaxed physical state.

The key is *shifting the mindset* from training for performance to exercising for health and enjoyment. Many ex-athletes eventually discover new ways to stay active that are gentler on the body and soul. For some, this means exploring sports and activities purely for recreation. For instance, a retired marathon runner might take up casual cycling with friends – feeling the wind on a weekend bike ride, enjoying the scenery without a stopwatch ticking. A former gymnast may fall in love with yoga, where movement is about flexibility and mindfulness rather than nailing a perfect score. There are stories of competitive weightlifters who, after retiring, tried Pilates or swimming to maintain strength and mobility in a low-impact way, and were surprised by how much they enjoyed being beginners in a different discipline. Embracing a "beginner's mind" in physical activities can actually be joyful for people who were once specialists. It's an opportunity to reconnect with the simple pleasure of movement, free from the pressure to win.

One illuminating example comes from a figure skater who, after hanging up her skates, felt a void where competition used to be. In her late 30s, she discovered a local CrossFit community and found that it offered just the right blend of camaraderie and challenge. The workouts were scaled to her ability, and she wasn't competing for medals – but her natural competitive spirit found a healthy outlet in trying to beat her own previous lift or sprint time. She noted that this community exercise allowed her to *channel her competitive nature* in a supportive environment, keeping her mentally and physically sharp. The weight of Olympic expectations was gone, but the endorphin rush and satisfaction of incremental progress remained. Whether it's CrossFit, weekend tennis matches, hiking clubs, or dance classes, there is life after elite sport in the form of *lifelong fitness activities*. These new routines can be social, fun, and adapted to an individual's evolving needs and limitations.

It's also important to address the toll that years of high-level sport can take on the body. Chronic injuries – a knee that never fully healed, a troublesome shoulder, the accumulated wear-and-tear of countless practices – often follow athletes into retirement. In the competitive years, athletes are conditioned to "push through" pain and ignore nagging injuries for the sake of performance. In retirement, however, the focus shifts to healing and long-term wellness. This might involve finally scheduling that surgery that was put off, committing to physical therapy without the rush to return by next season, or integrating rest days that were once unthinkable. Listening to one's body becomes paramount. As one sports medicine expert advises retiring athletes: *your body has been your instrument and sometimes your adversary – now it needs to become your partner in health.* If a former basketball player wakes up with aching joints, the goal is no longer to hit the court regardless, but to tend to those joints – maybe through low-impact swimming that day or therapeutic exercises to strengthen surrounding muscles.

Self-care is not just physical. The intense exercise of an athletic career does more than build muscle – it also regulates mood and stress through neurochemical benefits. When that level of activity drops, some athletes experience dips in mood or energy. The science behind this is well established: regular physical activity boosts natural mood enhancers like endorphins and serotonin, which reduce tension and anxiety. Fortunately, you don't need Olympian-level training to get these benefits. Studies show even moderate exercise – like 20-30 minutes of activity per day – can improve mood and calm the mind for hours afterwards. In retirement, an athlete can harness this knowledge to maintain mental health. If you're feeling the blues creeping in, a simple brisk walk or a light workout can trigger a familiar sense of well-being. It may not be the intense "runner's high" of competition days, but it's a sustainable *exercise high* that supports mental equilibrium. In fact, many former athletes begin to appreciate exercise in a new light: as a gift to themselves rather than a job. One retired skier mused that *for the first time since childhood, I'm moving my body just because it feels good, not because I have to hit a quota of laps or lifts.* This shift – from extrinsic motivation (winning, records) to intrinsic motivation (health, enjoyment) – can restore a sense of balance with one's body.

There is also the aspect of managing long-term health conditions that might have arisen from years of sports. Research has noted that retired athletes can be at risk for issues like osteoarthritis (from wear on joints) or metabolic changes if they drastically reduce activity. Being proactive about healthcare in this phase is crucial. Regular check-ups, consulting specialists for chronic injuries, and being mindful of nutrition as calorie needs change are all part of a good transition. On the flip side, studies have also found that former athletes often carry some health advantages into later life, such as better aerobic capacity or reduced risk of certain diseases, due to their history of fitness. By adopting a sustainable exercise routine, retired athletes can *capitalize on those advantages* and mitigate the negatives. For example, an ex-endurance athlete might not train 100 miles a week anymore, but continuing to do moderate cardio exercise can help maintain a healthy heart and weight.

Ultimately, the goal is to redefine fitness as a lifelong ally. It's about shifting the narrative: your body is not an engine solely for winning; it's the vessel that will carry you through a rich, long life. Treat it kindly. Enjoy its capabilities at a gentler pace. An athlete who once pursued "competitive perfection" can learn to embrace *holistic well-being.* If you need rest, take it without guilt – you've earned it. If an old injury flares up, acknowledge it and care for it, rather than feeling frustration. This compassionate approach prevents burnout and promotes longevity. Many retired athletes come to relish the fact that they can exercise on their own terms – no coaches' commands, no competitions looming – just the simple reward of staying healthy. They remain active well into middle and older age not because they have to, but because it keeps them connected to a core part of themselves: the love of movement. By designing a balanced routine that might include aerobic workouts for heart health, strength training for muscle and bone health (albeit far lighter than competitive days), and flexibility or mindfulness practices for recovery, athletes ensure that *fitness remains a source of strength and joy.* In turn, this supports their mental health, giving them structure and those familiar mood boosts, which are especially valuable in the often-unstructured life after sport. In summary, life after the medal isn't about abandoning the athletic lifestyle – it's about *adapting it* to serve one's well-being for the long haul.

Defining Your Legacy

In the final analysis of an athletic career, numbers and titles tell only part of the story. Gold medals, championship rings, records in the books – these are the accolades often highlighted in headlines and history. But when the stadium lights go dark, a deeper question emerges for the athlete: What do I want my life's story to be beyond the record books? Defining your legacy is a profoundly personal exercise, and retirement is the perfect time to take ownership of it. Rather than letting others or the media define who you are ("champion, gold medalist, record-holder"), you have the opportunity to shape a legacy that reflects *your values, your impact, and the entirety of your journey.*

One way to think of legacy is as the narrative you would want someone to tell about you decades from now. Early in an athlete's career, that narrative is often written by others – sports commentators, journalists, fans – focusing on athletic achievements. Now, *you become the author of your own story.* A helpful practice suggested by sports psychologists and life coaches is to write down your personal definition of success and legacy. This might include facets like family, community involvement, happiness, personal growth, and contribution to society. By broadening the definition of success, athletes can see that their sporting accomplishments are one chapter, but not the whole book. For example, an Olympian might write that she wants to be remembered not just as a world-class runner, but as a mentor who advanced opportunities for girls in sports and as a dedicated mother and friend. Another might define his legacy as being an innovator – perhaps he introduced a new technique to his sport that changed how future generations compete, and later he became an ambassador for fitness in schools. These personal reflections shift the focus from what you did to who you are and whom you affected.

It can be empowering to realize that *legacy is not solely measured in medals.* In truth, legacy often has more to do with character and influence. History is full of athletes whose post-competition lives made as much impact as their athletic feats. Think of the champion boxer who, after hanging up the gloves, became a humanitarian activist fighting for peace

148

and philanthropy. Or the Olympic gymnast who pioneered safer training techniques – her legacy living on in the wellbeing of athletes who came after. Some sports legends have even reinvented themselves in entirely new domains: a star player who becomes a successful entrepreneur or a political leader, contributing to society in ways that eclipse their sporting fame. By citing these examples (even anonymously), one sees that a sporting legacy can be just the opening act of a much larger life story.

At a more down-to-earth level, many athletes find that *the most cherished parts of their legacy are the human connections and values they carried forward.* An academic perspective on happiness throughout life found that close relationships – far more than fame or wealth – are what keep people fulfilled as years go by. In light of that, an athlete might consider how their legacy includes being a loving spouse, parent, or friend. The camaraderie of the locker room often translates into a lifelong habit of forging strong bonds; maintaining and prioritizing those relationships beyond sport can be a conscious part of one's legacy. Likewise, contributing to community can be deeply satisfying: perhaps you'll be remembered as the local hero who always showed up at charity events or who built a community center for kids. These acts weave you into the fabric of others' stories and ensure that your impact resonates beyond personal accolades.

Another element of legacy is the *causes or principles* you stand for. Many athletes have used their platform to advocate for something meaningful – whether it's mental health awareness, social justice, environmental causes, or education. If there is a cause close to your heart, championing it can become a hallmark of how you're remembered. For instance, a retired athlete who becomes a prominent spokesperson for mental health in sports (perhaps inspired by her own challenges) will be remembered for changing attitudes and possibly policies in her sport. In doing so, she transforms her legacy from one of athletic prowess to one of social impact. Similarly, an athlete who always valued sportsmanship might choose to get involved in initiatives that promote fair play and integrity in youth sports, thereby *shaping the culture* of the sport for the better. These contributions often stand the test of time more than records, because they continue to affect lives and norms long after the athlete's last game.

Consider also how an athlete might want to be seen as a well-rounded individual. During a sports career, life can be one-dimensional by necessity – all about the game, the training, the next win. Retirement offers a chance (and perhaps a challenge) to develop other dimensions of identity. Some ex-athletes dive into creative pursuits: art, music, writing memoirs or novels. Others travel the world or engage in business ventures. Every new endeavor adds layers to one's legacy. A person who was once known *only* as an athlete can evolve into a multi-faceted figure: an entrepreneur, an artist, a community leader, a scholar – the possibilities are endless. By succeeding (and even failing and learning) in multiple domains, athletes prove that their talents and drive were never confined to the sports field. They send a powerful message that reinvention is possible, and in doing so, they inspire others facing life transitions. One retired Paralympian, for example, went back to university in her 40s to earn a graduate degree and later became a cutting-edge researcher in disability technology – her legacy now bridges sport and science, showing the world that a champion's mindset can innovate far beyond competition.

When crafting a personal legacy, it is also helpful to remember that *how you make people feel* will be a huge part of how you are remembered. Teammates might not recall every statistic, but they will recall if you were a generous leader or a relentless competitor, and those anecdotes will be part of your legend. In your post-sport life, the same holds true: colleagues, family, and community members will remember the kindness, dedication, and passion you bring to your endeavors. Consciously aligning your actions with your core values ensures that this intangible part of your legacy is positive. For instance, if generosity is a value, perhaps your legacy includes not just charitable donations but also the generosity of spirit – mentoring without seeking credit, celebrating others' successes, and graciously sharing the spotlight.

In practical terms, shaping your legacy could involve setting down some concrete goals for this next phase that reflect your broader definition of success. You might list goals such as: *spend quality time with family and repair any relationships strained by years of focus on sport; achieve a non-sport career milestone like completing a degree or launching a business; contribute to a community project; mentor X number of young athletes over the next decade; maintain physical health to enjoy activities with future grandchildren,* and so on. These are not one-time goals like winning a race; they are ongoing commitments that build a life of meaning. Achieving them will require the same planning and dedication once devoted to training – but now the "coach" is your own inner values guiding you. Research on life satisfaction suggests that finding purpose and staying engaged in meaningful activities is vital for well-being in retirement. In other words, *defining and pursuing your legacy is not just about how others will remember you, but how you experience your own life going forward.* It gives you a reason to get up each day with intention and enthusiasm.

As this chapter draws toward a close, it becomes clear that a sporting legacy is just one chapter of a person's story, not the entire plot. The end of an athletic career, while sometimes bittersweet, offers the chance to consciously design a legacy that encompasses *all that you are.* By focusing on values like integrity, generosity, growth, and community impact, athletes often find a deep contentment and pride in the life they build after the medal podium. They realize that while a medal is hung around the neck for a moment, a legacy is carried in the hearts of others for years. In taking control of that narrative, athletes can ensure that how they are remembered outside the competitive arena truly reflects their fullest self – as champions not only in sport, but in life. This empowering outlook prepares the stage for the concluding chapter, which will tie together all these threads – identity, purpose, mental health, and legacy – into a cohesive vision of a fulfilling life beyond sport. With the right mindset and support, life after the final win can be rich, meaningful, and indeed, *a new kind of victory.*

Chapter 10

Beyond the Podium – Embracing a Fulfilling Future

Redefining Victory on Your Terms

Victory in sports is traditionally defined by podium finishes and gold medals – the moments of glory under bright lights. But life beyond the podium demands a new definition of success, one that you create for yourself. It's common for elite athletes to feel an emotional crash after achieving their highest goals; the so-called "podium hangover" can leave a void where purpose used to be. In fact, psychological research on Olympians has documented this post-victory emptiness. One record-breaking Olympic champion described the aftermath of the Games as a "traumatic emptiness," an incredible crash marked by the haunting question: *"Who am I outside of the swimming pool?"*. This post-competition comedown isn't rare – nearly 80% of Olympians may experience some form of post-Olympic depression, according to that athlete's estimation. Studies confirm that many athletes face mental health struggles after the high-stakes competition ends: about 24% of Olympians reported psychological distress following the Games, and those winding down their careers often suffer even more, as they grapple with a perceived *loss of goals and identity*. Clearly, chasing medals alone does not guarantee lasting happiness or self-worth.

The good news is that this empty feeling is not the end of your story – it's a turning point. To move forward, it helps to challenge the notion that victory only means standing on a podium. Yes, medals celebrate one kind of success, but your life is much richer and more expansive than any single competition. True victory can also be found in everyday personal achievements and the broader tapestry of your life. It's time to redefine success on your own terms. This means identifying what genuinely matters to you *as a person*, beyond what coaches, sponsors, or fans have traditionally valued.

Victory on your terms might look like:

- *Conquering everyday challenges* that once intimidated you (for example, overcoming a long-held fear or learning a new skill you never had time for during your athletic career).

- *Achieving life goals that bring you joy and meaning* – perhaps nurturing a loving family, contributing to your community, pursuing higher education, or excelling in a new career path outside of sports.

These are wins that no stopwatch can measure. By celebrating small victories – like mastering a hobby or volunteering to help others – you remind yourself that growth and progress continue in life after sports. And by striving for big-picture successes – like building a happy home or finding purpose in a second career – you create a new legacy that is uniquely yours. Such accomplishments may not come with trophies, but they can deliver profound satisfaction and pride.

Consider the story of one gymnastics champion who stepped back from the Olympic spotlight to put her mental well-being first. After years of defining herself through medals, she made the courageous choice to withdraw from a high-profile competition when her mind and body were telling her something was wrong. What happened next was extraordinary: an outpouring of support from teammates, fans, and the public at large. This athlete realized, in her own words, that the love she received *"made me realize I'm more than my accomplishments and gymnastics"*. She admitted that she had never truly believed that before. In that revelation, victory was redefined – it was no longer about scoring a 10.0 or impressing judges, but about honoring her own worth as a human being. Her *self-worth* finally extended beyond the tally of medals, and that insight proved more liberating than any podium moment.

Another former Olympian found that after the medal ceremonies were over, the moments that brought him the deepest happiness were surprisingly personal: cooking dinner with his family, hiking in nature, and waking up without the pressure of being "the best" every day. He described feeling *more joy in those simple experiences than he ever did winning a world championship*. This doesn't mean that competition wasn't important – it simply illustrates that life offers *many kinds of fulfillment*. By reflecting on what truly matters to you – not to sponsors, not to spectators or national federations – you can set new metrics for a fulfilling life. Maybe intellectual growth, friendships, or creative pursuits will become your new "gold medals." Perhaps giving back to your community or spending quality time with loved ones will feel like championship moments. There is no wrong answer when you define victory for yourself. The key is that your definition aligns with your values and passions, rather than external expectations.

Importantly, choosing your own definition of success is not just a feel-good exercise – it has real benefits for your mental health. Psychology research shows that when we are motivated by intrinsic goals (our inner values and interests) rather than extrinsic rewards (like fame, money, or approval), we tend to be happier and mentally healthier. In sports, athletes who find personal meaning and joy in what they do – independent of medals or praise – fare better emotionally. Studies have shown that intrinsic motivation contributes to improved psychological well-being in athletes. In contrast, if one's self-worth hinges entirely on external achievements, it can be a shaky foundation. When those external sources of validation dry up – as they inevitably do when competition ends or the applause fades – an athlete can feel lost or anxious. Many retired competitors struggle initially because all their life they felt valued "only if I win." Now, freed from that narrow definition, you have a chance to cultivate a more stable, resilient sense of self.

By redefining victory on your terms, you protect yourself from that post-competition crash. Instead of feeling that you peaked on the podium and life is downhill from there, you realize that life itself is a vast arena with countless opportunities to win. Overcoming the internal fear of starting something new is a win. Daring to be a beginner again in a new field is a win. Being present for your family and friends in ways you couldn't during your elite training days is a win. These victories might not generate headlines, but they generate something far more important:

inner fulfillment and a sustainable sense of purpose. Remember, the medals on your shelf commemorate one chapter of your life – a chapter of extraordinary dedication and talent. Now you get to write the next chapters, and in them, *you* decide what triumph looks like. It might be measured in laughter, in learning, or in loving and being loved. When you claim the right to define victory for yourself, you reclaim your life from the narrow confines of competitive results. That is a victory no one can ever take away from you – and it will fuel you for years to come.

The Champion Within – Confidence Beyond Competition

Retiring from sport or stepping away from competition doesn't mean you leave behind the qualities that made you an elite athlete. On the contrary, those qualities live within you, ready to be repurposed for new challenges. Think of it as an "inner champion" that still resides in your heart and mind. This inner champion is not about trophies or titles – it's the confidence, grit, and perseverance you earned through years of training and competition. That champion within is yours for life.

During your athletic career, you honed incredible strengths: discipline in your daily routines, the courage to perform under pressure, the resilience to bounce back from defeat, and the commitment to continuous improvement. These traits do not vanish once you hang up your jersey; they are part of your character. Now, beyond the arena, you can call on that same champion mindset in everyday life. Facing a daunting project at work? You know how to break down big goals into small steps – you've done it countless times in training. Confronting a health setback or recovering from an injury? You've learned how to endure pain, seek help from experts, and slowly rebuild – skills that directly translate to overcoming illness or physical challenges. Even something as simple as learning to live in the moment and enjoy the present can be approached with the mindset of an athlete: with focus, practice, and patience. Your competitive days have equipped you with an inner toolkit that can help you thrive in any environment.

It helps to consciously acknowledge this transferable skill set. One retired two-time gold medalist, for example, initially felt adrift after a career-ending injury. She wondered, "Who am I without my game?" But when she reflected on it, she realized that her original love for the sport and the skills learned on the field – teamwork, leadership, strategic thinking – could guide her in a new direction. She pivoted to a career in coaching and motivational speaking, using her platform to raise awareness about athlete mental health. In her words, the *same strategies and mindsets that help people succeed in sports are often transferable to business* and other endeavors. In other words, she discovered that the champion within her could shine outside of competition, too, once she applied those strengths to new goals.

You can do the same. Take stock of what your athletic journey has given you internally. Maybe you have an extraordinary ability to stay calm and focused under stress – that's a champion's poise which can make you a great emergency room nurse, a steadfast entrepreneur, or a rock for your family during tough times. Maybe you thrive on routine and self-discipline – that can help you stick to a study schedule if you pursue education, or maintain fitness and health in your everyday life, inspiring those around you. The confidence that comes from knowing you've done hard things, overcome pain, and emerged stronger is an asset you carry forward. It's like a flame that never goes out; you can ignite it whenever life demands perseverance.

Yet, many athletes struggle with confidence after retiring because they feel their source of validation has disappeared. In competition, you had a clear scoreboard, regular feedback from coaches, and applause from crowds to affirm your abilities. Now, in everyday life, applause is rare. This is where a crucial shift in mindset occurs: learning to derive confidence from within, rather than from external praise. Psychological insights into self-esteem suggest that if you base your self-worth entirely on external validation – like medals, rankings, or audience approval – you set yourself up for emotional instability. Researchers have found that *contingent self-esteem* (self-esteem dependent on external approval or achievements) can lead to higher anxiety, stress, and even depression when those external sources vanish. Think about it: an athlete who only feels "good enough" when hearing the roar of a crowd might feel profound emptiness when the stadium goes quiet. The remedy is to cultivate a stable sense of confidence that doesn't rely on others' applause.

Start by recognizing your worth as a person, not just as a performer. You are not only "valuable" when you win a race; you are valuable, period. Remind yourself of the qualities that make you a strong and unique individual – qualities that were there long before you won any medals. Perhaps it's your determination, your creativity, your kindness, or your curiosity to learn. These traits define you more deeply than any stopwatch time. It may help to practice *personal affirmations*: literally telling yourself, in your internal dialogue, that you are proud of the effort you put into a task, regardless of the outcome. Many former athletes find it useful to set small daily goals and then give themselves credit for each one achieved, creating a new kind of "scoreboard" that reflects personal growth. For example, you might decide, "Today I will spend one hour preparing for that job interview," or "I will go for a morning run to take care of my health." When you accomplish it, acknowledge it – perhaps not with a gold medal, but with a moment of satisfaction and maybe sharing the achievement with a loved one. Over time, these habits of affirming yourself build a resilient self-esteem.

Also, remember that you don't have to go it alone. In sports, you likely had teammates, coaches, and supporters. In life beyond sports, meaningful relationships can be your new cheering squad. Friends, family, mentors, or fellow retired athletes can provide encouragement and remind you of your strengths when you doubt yourself. Whereas in competition you might have heard a stadium cheer, now you can cherish the quieter but deeper affirmations from people who care about you. A compliment from a colleague, a thank-you from someone you helped, or a heartfelt conversation with a friend can all reinforce your sense that you are contributing value to the world. Lean into those connections. Psychologically, we know that a sense of belonging and support is a powerful pillar for one's self-esteem and confidence.

One powerful metaphor is to view yourself not as a "former champion" but as a champion of your own life. That means carrying yourself with the same dignity and self-belief that you did as an athlete, even though you're in a different arena now. Your arena might be a classroom, a boardroom, a creative studio, or your home – wherever it is, approach challenges there with the mindset that *"I've conquered challenges before, I can conquer this too."* That inner champion voice might sound like the coach in your head that used to push you to do one more rep or to not quit when things got hard. Now, it can push you to send out another job application after a rejection, or to remain patient and positive during a long recovery from an injury. It's the same voice that says, "Keep going – you've got this," just applied to new circumstances.

And if moments arise when you truly feel lost, remember that even during your sports career, confidence was not a constant, unbroken feeling. You had slumps, bad days, maybe even crises of confidence, but you found ways to rebound – often by returning to basics, seeking guidance, or adjusting your approach. You can do the same now. If your confidence falters, go back to basic principles: take care of your health, set a small achievable task, talk to a supportive friend or counselor, and build back up step by step. You have a well of resilience to draw from. As a matter of fact, research in personal development suggests that self-confidence built on experience and competence is more stable than glory-based self-esteem. Achievements that you earned through effort can't be easily taken away from you. Each time you draw on a skill you mastered or a lesson you learned in sports, you reinforce the belief *"I can do this, because I've done hard things before."* Psychologist Albert Bandura's concept of self-efficacy aligns with this – it's the confidence in one's ability to succeed in specific situations, and it grows every time you overcome a challenge. So, each new obstacle you tackle in post-sport life, no matter how small, is actually an opportunity to reinforce your inner champion's confidence.

In sum, you are still the champion you always were, even without a uniform or a medal around your neck. The form of competition has changed – now you compete against yesterday's self, aiming to be a stronger, wiser, or kinder person today – but the champion's spirit is unchanged. Trust in that. By grounding your confidence in who you are and what you can do (rather than what others think of you), you carry an unshakeable strength into everything you pursue. The applause has faded, but in its place is something far more enduring: the voice inside that says "I believe in myself." That voice, that inner champion, will lead you to victories in all chapters of your life.

Inspiring the Next Generation

As you work through your post-competition journey, remember that it isn't just *your* future that you're influencing – you are also shaping a legacy for those who come after you. In elite sports, we often talk about "leaving a legacy." Usually that brings to mind records set or medals won. But there's a deeper kind of legacy you can offer: being a role model in how to handle the transition out of sport with honesty, balance, and courage. By openly embracing mental health and a well-rounded life, you can inspire the next generation of athletes in a way that goes far beyond your athletic accomplishments.

Today's young competitors are watching their heroes closely. When active champions like yourself show that it's okay to prioritize mental well-being, it sends a powerful message to up-and-coming athletes: *your mental health matters as much as your training.* In recent years, this message has started to echo across the sporting world. High-profile athletes have broken the silence about their own post-competition struggles, prompting a shift in attitudes. For example, one world-renowned gymnast's candor about her mental health challenges prompted sports organizations worldwide to pay attention. In the lead-up to the 2024 Olympics, several national teams began preparing resources to help their athletes handle the post-Olympic blues, precisely because they saw what happened when even the most successful athletes struggled after the spotlight moved on. Sports psychologists and coaches are increasingly gearing up to support athletes *after* the medals are awarded, not just during competition, and that's largely thanks to athletes who bravely spoke up about their experiences.

By embracing your own "podium hangover" journey and then sharing what you learned, you become a beacon for others. Imagine a young athlete who idolized you during your career. Yes, they remember your victories, but now they also see you as a whole human being. When you speak openly about how you dealt with identity loss or depression after retirement – and how you rebuilt your life – you give that young athlete permission to acknowledge their own emotions without shame. You become living proof that one can be a champion in sport and also vulnerable, real, and proactive about mental health. This is a *profoundly impactful example.* It challenges the old stereotype that athletes must be

163

invincible machines. Instead, you're showing that strength includes acknowledging when you need help or when you feel uncertain, and that doing so is actually a sign of wisdom, not weakness.

Many retired athletes have already started turning their personal challenges into fuel for change. Some have become outspoken advocates for mental health policy changes in sports. They've lobbied for things like mandatory mental health resources in athletic programs, or "mental health baseline" screenings for collegiate and pro athletes – akin to how concussion baseline tests are done – so that any post-competition mood changes can be caught and addressed early. In one illustrative case, a former Olympian who recognized the "unhealthy system" that left athletes unprepared for real life pushed for reforms to give athletes a greater voice in sports organizations. Others are working behind the scenes to change the culture at sports academies and clubs, encouraging these institutions to teach young athletes about life beyond sport and to allow time for education, family, and personal development alongside training. Every time a retired athlete speaks up to a governing body or joins a committee to improve athlete welfare, they light the way for future sports policies that treat athletes as whole people, not just medal-producing machines.

Perhaps an even more direct way retired athletes inspire the next generation is through mentorship. You have a wealth of experience that extends beyond how to perfect a jump shot or a gymnastics routine – you've learned life lessons the hard way. By mentoring younger athletes, you can guide them to develop a more holistic identity from the start. For example, one former professional football player, after retiring early due to injury, found a new calling in mentoring college athletes on mental health and identity. He was hired by a university to share his story and support student-athletes in understanding that their worth isn't solely tied to sport. In speaking with them, he emphasizes the importance of vulnerability and balance. He even tells them that the painful process he went through – of finding out who he was outside of football – turned out to be a "blessing in disguise," because it taught him that he is *"more than an athlete"*. Those words, coming from a sports hero, resonate deeply with young players. It reassures them that if one day they can't play, life will go on and can even be great – and it motivates them to cultivate interests and skills beyond the field.

Similarly, other retired athletes have started programs or companies dedicated to helping their peers with transition. A former Olympian in track might host workshops for national team members on career planning, or a retired NBA player might fund scholarships for athletes to finish their degrees. One former professional athlete founded a transition support service that works with players before they retire, coaching them on how to prepare for that major life change. These kinds of efforts create a ripple effect: the next generation sees that preparing for life beyond sport is just part of being a champion. It normalizes the idea that an athletic career has a *sunset*, and that's not something to dread but something to plan for and embrace.

Your personal journey of overcoming the post-competition crash is part of this bigger movement. Every time you share an insight or lend a hand to a young athlete, you are contributing to a healthier sports culture. You might do it in a very public way – like speaking at a conference or on social media about mental health – or in an intimate way, like advising a younger teammate over coffee. No act is too small. Even a casual conversation where you acknowledge to a young gymnast, swimmer, or runner that "hey, it's okay to feel nervous or sad; I've been there too," can be life-changing for them. You're lighting a path that you yourself might have wished to see when you were rising through the ranks.

It's a proud and forward-looking role to take on. Think of it this way: your gold medals eventually will gather dust, records may be broken by others, and the fame of your athletic prowess will inevitably fade with time – that's just the nature of sports. But the impact you have on real people's lives, especially young athletes' lives, can last for generations. An athlete you mentor today might go on to mentor others tomorrow, continuing the chain. A policy you advocate for today might protect countless athletes ten years from now from suffering in silence. This legacy of compassion and wisdom is as significant as any championship. In fact, many athletes find it even more rewarding. As one legendary swimmer-turned-mental-health-advocate noted, helping others find hope and balance has given him a new sense of purpose as powerful as winning gold.

Importantly, inspiring the next generation doesn't mean you have all the answers or have a perfect life (no one does). It simply means you're willing to lead by example in growth. You show that it's possible to transition, to struggle, and to come out the other side stronger and happier. You show that an athlete's story doesn't have to end at retirement – it can transform and continue in wonderful new forms. By doing this, you help young athletes see *the long game*. They start to understand that their sports career, no matter how glittering, is just one part of a long life. And with that understanding, they can approach sports with a healthier mindset, maybe avoiding some of the pitfalls of over-identification and burnout that earlier generations faced. In short, your journey beyond the podium lights the way for those still climbing the podium. It teaches them that mental well-being is as crucial as physical training and that a life in balance is the ultimate achievement.

Sports psychology experts have taken notice of these changes and are backing them up. Recent research reviews conclude that athletes should be better prepared for retirement through life skills training and transition programs. This is exactly what you are advocating by living your truth. The sporting world is slowly realizing that developing a champion *in life* is just as important as developing a champion on the field. You are at the forefront of that change. By turning your post-competition challenges into wisdom and sharing it, you not only heal yourself – you pave a smoother road for all the champions to come.

Embracing Life's Marathon

Life beyond the medal podium is often described as a new chapter, but perhaps a more fitting analogy is that it's the start of an ultimate marathon – one that lasts the rest of your life. Unlike a 100m sprint or a single season, this marathon isn't about outrunning anyone else. It's a personal journey of continuous growth, discovery, and fulfillment. As you stand at this juncture, it's time to approach life with the same passion and determination you once brought to sport, but with a new perspective: this time the goal is not to be the best in the world at something, but to become the best version of yourself.

Embracing life's marathon means understanding that there will be uphill stretches and easy coasting periods, times when you feel exhilarated and times when you feel exhausted – and that's okay. In sports, you learned to pace yourself for the race; now you will pace yourself for the long journey of life. There is no finish line you're racing toward, which is liberating. It means you can continually set new goals and checkpoints that matter to you. Instead of one giant goal (like an Olympic event every four years), you'll have evolving goals – perhaps running a local marathon for charity next year, then learning a musical instrument the year after, then starting a small business at some point, and so on. Each goal gives you something to strive for, but you also have the wisdom to know that it's about the journey, not just the destination.

Many former athletes come to find that their "second act" in life can be every bit as satisfying as their sports career, if not more so. During your athletic years, life may have been thrilling but also narrow in focus – everything revolved around training and competing. Now, the world opens up. One retired champion described his post-sports life as an adventure where he finally had the chance to explore all the interests and dimensions of himself that were on hold for so long. He threw himself into learning new languages, traveling, and even took up painting – endeavors he never had time for in his swimming days. To his surprise, he found the same joy in mastering a simple landscape painting as he once did standing on a podium, because it was *his* accomplishment in his own personal journey. Another athlete, who had been a record-breaking sprinter, shared that while nothing could replace the thrill of competition, the sense of peace and contentment she eventually cultivated in her post-athlete life felt "deeper and more lasting" than the high of victory. She talked about how overcoming the identity crisis and building a new life was *itself* a monumental achievement – one that she regards as equal to, if not greater than, her Olympic medals.

These stories underscore a powerful point: the challenges you are overcoming right now – redefining yourself, restoring your mental health, finding new purpose – are heroic feats in their own right. They may not come with a certificate or a news headline, but consider the courage it takes to start over, the endurance required to push through emotional lows, and the vision needed to reinvent oneself. In a very real sense, you are conquering something as formidable as any opponent or world record: you are conquering the challenge of life after the pinnacle of sport. Give yourself credit for every step forward in this marathon. Did you wake up one morning feeling directionless, but still manage to get up and explore a new opportunity? That's a win. Did you battle through feelings of inadequacy in a beginner's class at university or an entry-level job, yet stick with it and improve? That's a victory. Over time, these victories accumulate into a meaningful life, much like miles accumulate in a marathon.

One strategy that many athletes find helpful in this long journey is to continue setting goals – but make them diverse and attuned to personal growth. During your sports career, your goals might have all been in one domain (e.g. strength, speed, skill in sport). Now, you can set goals across various domains of life: maybe a fitness goal (staying active but for health/enjoyment rather than competition), a career goal (starting at the bottom of a new field and working your way up), a relationship goal (reconnecting with friends you lost touch with, or being an present parent/partner), and a self-development goal (like learning or improving at a hobby). Setting these goals gives you direction and the thrill of progress. And unlike the zero-sum nature of competitive sports (where only one can get gold), in life's marathon everyone can win their own race. There is no limit to how much happiness or accomplishment is "allowed." You'll find that cheering on others in their life journeys – just as you now inspire younger athletes – brings its own joy, without detracting from your own path.

It's also important to remember to enjoy the run. In an athletic race, you might not have had the luxury to slow down and soak in the environment – but in the marathon of life, you absolutely can. Take time to appreciate the everyday pleasures that perhaps you missed while training. Maybe that's enjoying a slow morning with a cup of coffee, now that you don't have a 5 AM drill. Maybe it's spending a leisurely weekend with your family, or saying yes to social invitations you once declined due to training schedules. These moments are not trivial; they are the fabric of a fulfilling life. Embrace new experiences with the curiosity of a beginner. Remember how, as an athlete, you sometimes experienced *flow*

— a state of being fully immersed and present, whether in a race or practice? You can find that flow in other activities now. Some ex-athletes report finding a similar "in the zone" feeling while doing things like gardening, writing, or hiking a mountain trail. It may be different in intensity, but it is rich in satisfaction because it's tied to *living life on your own terms.*

As you navigate this marathon, take care of your mental and physical well-being as diligently as you did in your sport – but adapt your methods to suit a balanced life. Physical activity, for instance, can remain a pillar of your routine, but now free of the pressure to perform. Staying active is proven to help stabilize mood and provide structure; indeed, suddenly stopping all exercise can increase the risk of depressive symptoms in former athletes. So run, bike, swim or do yoga – do it for enjoyment and health. This keeps your body engaged and those familiar endorphins flowing, which can ward off the blues. At the same time, allow yourself to rest and recover. During your competitive days, rest was merely a means to an end (recovery for the next competition). Now, rest is an end in itself – a reward you've earned to savor life. Sleep in when you need to, take vacations without guilt, let your mind and body rejuvenate. After years of intense scheduling, unstructured downtime might feel strange, but it is in these unscheduled moments that you often discover new interests or insights.

A retired Olympic goalkeeper shared a piece of advice that resonates here. She said: *"At the end of the day, the Olympics part of your life will end. You have a lot of time for the other parts."* In other words, athletic glory, no matter how great, occupies a relatively short span of a lifetime. After that, you potentially have decades filled with "other parts" – family, second and third careers, personal growth, community involvement, etc. Embrace those parts with the same enthusiasm you once reserved for sport. Think of life as a series of seasons: your season as an athlete was spectacular, and now new seasons await that can be just as rewarding in different ways. Some retired athletes, looking back in their elder years, even say that their post-sport life was more satisfying because it was more *balanced*. They got to experience the full range of what life has to offer, from the mundane to the magical, without being confined to a singular identity.

As you run this marathon of life, don't be afraid to occasionally look back and acknowledge how far you've come. The finish line of your sports career was not the end – it was a checkpoint. Since then, you've grown in resilience and wisdom. Perhaps you've overcome emotional struggles, discovered new passions, or simply learned to *be* without constantly doing. Those are immense achievements. In a way, you are still accumulating medals – but these medals are internal. Each represents something like "Overcame my self-doubt," "Found joy in helping others," "Maintained my wellbeing," or "Started a new venture at 40." Imagine lining those medals up on a shelf; they tell the story of a life fully lived.

Ultimately, remember that the podium was only one stage of your journey. You stood there and it was glorious, but life has many stages and many forms of podiums. You might stand on a stage at a university graduation receiving a degree, or on a small podium giving a speech about your experiences, or figuratively "on the podium" when your child celebrates a success that you guided them toward. The end of competitive sport is not the end of *winning*. It's the beginning of a new kind of competition – not against others, but against your own limitations and fears, in pursuit of personal excellence and happiness. And in this competition, the rules are kinder: you can win every day, and so can everyone around you.

Life's marathon is to be embraced, not endured. You have already proven you can conquer challenges and reach goals; now your task is to apply that prowess to the grand adventure of living. There will be surprises along the way, setbacks and triumphs, but you are equipped to handle them. When you feel unsure, just remember the central lesson of this chapter: the greatest victory of all is a life well-lived beyond the medals. With your redefined sense of success, your inner champion's confidence, and your commitment to ongoing growth, you are poised to conquer the wider world. And unlike a race that ends with a tape at the finish line, this journey keeps offering new horizons. Your greatest win might still be ahead of you – not in the form of a medal, but in the form of peace of mind, love, purpose, and the knowledge that you have become so much more than what any podium could represent. That is a victory truly worth celebrating, for a lifetime.

Epilogue

The anthem fades, the lights dim, and the calendar turns. The body knows how to chase; the mind learns how to stay. This book traced the quiet hours after the roar, when triumph can feel like a trap and confidence can slip through tired fingers. The lesson is simple: medals mark a moment; meaning grows from practice.

Training once aimed at fractions of a second; now attention shifts to the shape of days. Recovery is not a pause, but a craft. Sleep becomes a skill. Food fuels more than splits. Breath softens the edges of thought. Conversations with teammates, family, and rivals open new rooms. Coaching emerges as partnership. Therapy becomes a gym for the inner life. Curiosity returns. So does play.

Identity widens. Champion remains a chapter, not the title of the whole book. Roles multiply: learner, mentor, builder, friend. The same discipline that sharpened performance now guards boundaries, honors rest, and keeps promises made off the track, court, pool, or mat. The scoreboard expands to include moments that never trend: reading to a child, holding a hand, showing up when cameras stay home.

There will be dips and long Tuesdays. Cravings for the rush will visit, as cravings do. On those days, reach for the tools practiced here: routines that anchor, questions that reframe, communities that hold, values that outlast applause. Train purpose the way sprints were trained—reps, feedback, patience. Trust that momentum can be built from quiet starts.

Winning once proved capacity. Living well proves continuity. The gift of high performance was never speed alone; it was attention, care, and the courage to begin again. The podium was never the finish line; it was a doorway. Step through, carry hard-won skills into the generous race of life, and let the next season shine brighter than any medal.